The Shaman Between Worlds

Spiritual Warrior Social Mediator

Daylight Publishing
With Lulu Publishing

Roy. E. Day Jr.

Edited and Cover by Helen Manget

TABLE OF CONTENTS

DEDICATION	2
INTRODUCTION	3
WORLDVIEW OF A HEALER	13
THE CIRCLE IS A SYMBOL OF LIFE	45
ARRIVING	62
SNOWY EARTH AND A SPIRITUAL HIERARCHY	77
THE FOUR DAY HEALING SWEAT LODGE	156
WARRIORS OF THE RAINBOW	228
THE FIRST SCHISM	253
THE SECOND SCHISM	287
FINDING THE STAR CHILD	300
CONCLUSION	323
BIBLIOGRAPHY	324

Dedication

Everything I write is for my family, friends, and this beautiful planet. This book is specifically dedicated to my spiritual teachers and those fellow travelers who were beside me on the spiritual or shamanic path, both those at home and the Northern Paiute and the River people, who welcomed me and helped heal me.

My spiritual teachers in order:

- Master Jack Johns – my first Karate teacher
- Ruth Stillman – theosophists – esoteric section, Co-Freemason – top 13 initiate
- Evelyn Monahan – taught parapsychology – GA State University
- Grandmother Evelyn Eaton – Metis Shaman – Co-Freemason – top 13 initiate
- Grandfather Raymond Stone – Northern Paiute Shaman – who avoided fame, publicity
- Dr. Gayle Pierce – Healer, Buddhist, friend of Dali Lama
- Master Robert Quinn – my Karate Sifu

The fellow travelers were my friends Tom and Debbie, my girlfriend Peggy, my brothers Stephen, Winslow and his girlfriend Fay, and sometimes friends from Theatrical Outfit, later Seven Stages.

Introduction

This paper is presented as a work of social science investigating shamanic ritual and changes of shamanic ritual in relation to cultural conflict and change. Fundamentally this is a story about people, a human drama whose main characters came from radically different cultural backgrounds to find and tread the path of the shaman. The setting of this story is eastern California; the time frame begins for the author in 1976, and continues into the present. The material setting is one of acculturation, Paiutes and Whites living and working in harmony. However, the ideological conflict that began with the intersection of European and Native American culture is an ongoing process. The traditional Native American view of Nature (and that of the shaman) conceives a world alive and filled with spirits and power. The modern world offers a mechanical, inanimate view of Nature to match the techno-industrial culture that exercises an assumed, biblically granted dominion over Nature. This vastly different viewpoint of the world is indicative of this unresolved ideological conflict.

The shaman - when defined in a general sense, not pertaining to a specific culture but as world-wide phenomenon - is a community recognized magical-religious specialist, who mediates on behalf of his client or community by inducing in himself an altered state of consciousness and then working with some form of magic or power to achieve a specific goal. This work is usually done in association with the human soul, with spirits, and a spirit world. The most basic concept to grasp for those who would understand the work of the shaman is that he is a spiritual go-between. His job, although seldom full-time, is that of a professional mediator and intermediary. The community as a whole or an individual client will come to the shaman seeking him to perform in one of his two modes of operation. He will be asked to work on behalf of the client(s) to bring about some desired condition or event, or to remove or prevent some undesired condition or event.

The shaman, by the nature of his direct experience with the spirits, power, and magic underlying observable reality, guided by the ancient, secret tradition of his people, is a spiritual mediator on behalf of the community as a whole and those individuals within it who have neither the direct experience nor knowledge to deal directly with such matters.

The shaman mediates on behalf of his client(s) to achieve their various goals in one of six traditional roles:

1) as a <u>healer</u>: as a master of spirits, as a curer,

2) as an exorcist, as a ritual specialist - as a <u>specialist of the soul</u> to retrieve the wandering or lost soul

3) to escort the dead to the realm of the dead

4) to communicate with spirits, gods, or the dead for various

reasons, such as finding a lost object,

5) to explore and journey in the realm of the soul

6) as the <u>charmer of game</u>: to find game, to render them submissive, to promote fertility and a bountiful subsistence

7) as a <u>beneficent sorcerer</u>: to work good magic, to defend against harmful sorcery

8) as a <u>malevolent sorcerer</u>: to perform magic with the intent to harm or bring suffering

9) As a <u>judicial sorcerer</u>: to act the instrument of justice, to carry out community approved retribution.

The Paiute shaman today smokes his sacred pipe, sings his spirit songs, works with one or more spirits, and utilizes his eagle feathers and other sacred objects to heal his patients, help his community, and to help the world as a whole. Usually this work is performed as ritual in a sweat lodge. With the exception of matches, a metal water bucket, and a metal water ladle, there is nothing in the sweat lodge ritual of today to separate it from man's pre-historical quest for spiritual meaning and power. The shaman of today sees himself much like his pre-historical predecessors, as a taker of grave risk in the performance of his craft. As a mediator dealing with spirits and power, the shaman believes himself to be taking serious risks of illness, of soul loss, and of death in the performance of his craft.

In self-image, by affirmation, and by activity the shaman is a spiritual warrior in a conflict between the forces of health and life against the forces of disease and death. In those instances involving contact with, communion with, or possession by a spirit or spirits, the shaman performs in a dual activity as both the performer of action and as the field of that activity. In a possibly more appropriate image, the shaman performs in a dual function as both warrior and battlefield.

In a point of contrast, the Paiute shaman of today speaks English as his primary language, drives a late model pick-up truck, and watches the same national news, the same programs and movies on TV as does that mythical "normal" American. This paradox and seeming conflict was not lost on James Downs who studied the Paiute's immediate neighbors to the west, the Washoe. What he wrote about the Washoe was so true of the Paiutes, as it would be of so many tribes, that in the following paraphrase I substituted their name. "A distinct Paiute material culture no longer exist...while the outward signs of Paiute culture have disappeared and the Paiute live in the world as it is, they have not abandoned their (traditional) identity. The other world of the Paiute is a world of the mind. The old tales are not forgotten...the belief in the nature of power in the universe is still very real. (Downs, 1968, p.109)."

Mircea Eliade, the father of shamanic study, would refer to an oral tradition or body of shamanic knowledge as the ancient secret tradition of such-and-such people. This term applies well to Native American shamanism. It is ancient, coming from a past unknown. It is secret, for those whom were chosen, by a shaman or by some significant life experience. It is a tradition, a sacred body of knowledge, passed orally from generation to generation.

The ancient secret tradition of Native Americans as a whole, and of the Paiutes in specific, espouses an understanding of Nature that stands in sharp contrast to that of mainstream modern American culture. Those who would seek the aid of the shaman, from whatever background, must face this contrast and may naturally look to the shaman's example for understanding. It is the shaman who mediates between his traditional world view and that of the materialistic, rational, science-based, White, Christian, dominant culture of modern America.

This contrast had been known and accepted by myself subconsciously for years, but was not consciously understood until I was introduced into a Paiute sweat lodge. The woman who brought me into the situation was a Canadian born poet, journalist, and author some fifty years my senior. The medicine man whose sweat lodge I attended was an ex-soldier, janitor, pipe carver, sculptor some forty years my senior.

Despite their widely differing backgrounds they had finished the four day fast that marked their graduation into the world of shamanism and full status as pipe healers together. These two were friends and colleagues who worked with each other and for each other in the ritual of their craft. In many ways this thesis is the story of their co-operation and their conflicts. This is not to ignore the factors making up the larger picture such as the history both of the nation and region, the history and world view of the cultures involved, and social conflicts and movements past and present. Indeed, the relationship and conflict between the main characters cannot be separated from that larger social picture but may serve to bring that larger picture into focus with more clarity and depth.

This paper focuses on three areas of social and ideological conflict in relation to the shaman, his ritual, and changes of that ritual. The three areas of conflict are presented as questions:

1) **Will the ancient secret tradition and practices remain secret and closed, or will they become more open, will they be shared with and open to non-natives?**

2) **What effect will Jesus and Christianity have on traditional belief and practice?**

3) **Will the impersonal and mechanical view of Nature promulgated by the dominant culture have an effect on traditional belief and practice?**

This thesis is ethnography of ritual and ritual change. It presents the contemporary shaman in a situation of acculturational conflict and change. The shaman is pictured as a spiritual warrior, one who fights a spiritual battle on behalf of others. This dual role of warrior and battlefield has a social parallel in social conflict because the shaman is both a public and influential member of his community. **This paper** postulates that in instances of acculturation the shaman in his dual role of spiritual and social mediator will reflect social change by change in ritual. Significant ideological change will be manifest in symbolic change. Symbols may be added, subtracted, or undergo a change in meaning. This postulate may be applicable to all forms of shamanism in situations of acculturation and ideological conflict except those primarily Asian forms which have become rigidly solidified over the passage of time and are limited an exact re-enactment of a myth or an inflexibly prescribed ritual.

Worldview of a Healer

This work is not meant to be autobiographical nor am I a central character in what is a factual drama. It is not melodramatic or exciting by American entertainment standards in that it contains sex or violence. Sex has little bearing to this story and what violence it contains is psychic. The story does deal in life and death struggles; primarily that of one woman against a cancer which failed to take her life.

It is a drama in that it deals in the strongest of emotions – love, betrayal, racial hatred, and forgiveness. To tell this story accurately I will relate it as I lived it. Those parts of this story that I didn't experience I have had communicated to me by more than one source or were derived from acknowledged literature.

I met Evelyn Eaton at a beautiful and isolated writer's retreat in the north Georgia mountains. I had been taken there with my girlfriend by an elderly friend and teacher, Ruth Stillman. I knew at that time that Ruth and Eve were associated through the society they referred to as the Co - Freemasons. This is an international offshoot of the Freemasons that allows the women and men to participate in the Masonic rituals together. In the world there were supposed to be a small (less than fourteen) and limited number of people who could attain the highest degree, with vacancies occurring with the passing away of one of that limited number. I knew that Ruth was one of that elite and highly-selected cabal; so was Eve. Ruth had brought me to Eve because in Ruth's terms, she was a medicine woman.

In 1972 at the age of eighteen I fell over a 100 ft. in a demolition event that took two lives. Despite the finest modern heath care the doctor's prognosis was that my legs would remain permanently paralyzed as a result of the fracture and natural fusion of my spinal column at T-12, L-1. Although I had never been much of a joiner or follower, I had always been interested in man's search for meaning and the great diversity of religious expression. My near-death and resultant injury had given me a new impetus in my search for meaning and added a new corollary interest in unconventional healing.

By the mid-seventies a group of interested people from the academic and theatrical world of Atlanta were getting together at my house once or twice a month to discuss and investigating mysticism, myth, and ritual and their potential for the heightening of awareness and as a stimulus in the healing process. We were independent in that we did not join, follow, or adhere to any specific set of beliefs; rather we studied a wide range of subjects including the beliefs and practices of the Native Americans.

It was through the investigations of this group that I came to know Ruth Stillman as a teacher and friend. She had brought me to

Eve to learn and be worked on.

Eve, as Ruth, was in her seventies. Eve was short, spry, and quick, with a cute "pug" face and a keen sense of humor. Ruth, Peggy, and I sat around with Eve in the living room of her cottage and talked about ourselves, about the plight and beliefs of the American Indian and about things spiritual. It was obvious then and became more obvious later that she was knowledgeable about the Eastern, Western, and shamanic spiritual traditions. She chose to use the symbols, the tools and the methods of the Native American shaman, but she could explain and relate them to the orthodox religions of the East and the pre-Christian religions of the West.

It was also immediately obvious that she believed in the principles of reincarnation and karma and that in her view she shared that belief with the traditional Native Americans.

After a long and pleasant conversation she began her healing work.

She began with a process she called smudging. She placed some sage inside a large shell and lit it. Once the flame was burning well she put out the fire and with the sage smoldering said a prayer something like she later taught me, "Great Spirit, we ask that You bless this smoke that it might cleanse and purify."

Then she sensed the room and everyone in it beginning with herself. She did this and taught us to do it, saying that censing for purification was in the Bible and a world-wide phenomenon We were instructed to use our hands and treat the smoke as though it were water, pulling it to us to cense our face, both sides, and then over our heads to cense our backs. After the first four movements we were to sense our whole bodies with similar movements. Eve then censed her sacred healing objects, her eagle feather fan and her healing stone. She passed each object over the smoke towards the six directions (E., S., W., N., up, and down.). She told us that smoke had always been used in such purification and that she preferred to use cedar bark or sage originating in the mountains or the desert.

As I sat there in my wheelchair she asked me just to relax and pray, and to try to be passive. She began to work on me with her healing fan, the large feathers of a bird of prey attached at the bottom making a fan that when swished through the air sounds remarkably like a large bird in flight. As she faced me and then moved around me she used first a rapid strong motion, that created a quick breeze and then a softer, gentler motion. She had used terms such as positive and negative energy and it immediately came to mind that she was removing the negative energy and replacing it with positive energy. She had used such terms as aura and energy field in our conversations, and I felt that she was working on them in order to heal my body. It was clear to me at the time that this was a woman with a wide field of knowledge who had come to adopt the practices of her native land, finding them powerful, meaningful, and not out of context with the other ancient traditions she had studied.

After she had worked her way around my body with her fan she worked on me with her healing stone. Her healing stone was circular and flat, about the size of her palm and from the nature of its smoothness had spent hundreds or thousands of years with water rushing over it. She used it by placing it on my body with her palm on top, on the top of my head, my forehead, and then my heart. She then ran it down the long bones on the front of my body. She then moved around behind me and had me lean forward. She pressed the stone against the top of my head, against my occipital crest and medulla oblongata, and then down my spine. She would hold the stone against me for between ten and thirty seconds, and when she moved it along my long bones, she moved it very slowly. She stood behind me after she finished with the rock. She stood with a hand on either shoulder, behind me in silence, for about five minutes. The entire healing treatment lasted over fifteen, but less than forty-five minutes.

Ruth had insisted that I bring some of the objects I had collected and she related that to Eve that I had brought some. My objects consisted of a rock and a crow feather I had brought wrapped inside a deerskin. The deerskin was from a faun I had found as a road kill and skinned. The rock had been given to me by Evelyn Monahan who was a psychic of national reputation and had taught parapsychology in non-credit, adult enrichment classes at Georgia State University. She had picked it up and brought it back to me during her trip to the Great Pyramid. I had found the crow feather by accident in the woods when I had been startled by a low flying crow and found the lone feather, standing almost upright in the pine straw. Eve liked all three stories and said I should consider the feather and stone as sacred healing objects and begin working with them. After some more conversation and pleasantries Eve invited us to visit again, telling me to bring whatever sacred objects I had, that she would bless them and instruct me in their use.

We finished the healing session and our visit by smoking the sacred pipe. Eve relit the sage and went through the smudging process with her pipe and its accessories. She smudged the tobacco, the matches, the straightened metal coat-hanger that is used to clean the pipe stem, the Joshua stick from the Joshua tree used to stir the fire inside the pipe bowl, the pipe stem, and the bowl of the pipe. This was done verbally, as she passed each object through the four directions, then up and down, she invoked the Powers of the East, South, West, North, and those of the Great Spirit, and the Earth Mother.

As she loaded the pipe I heard the same beautiful invocation I was to hear so often, not exactly the same words, but always the same intent. She loaded the pipe and used it in much the same manner as that described by Black Elk in Joseph Epes Brown's book, <u>The Sacred Pipe.</u> The first pinch of tobacco was held up and offered to the Great Spirit and placed inside the bowl of the red stone pipe.

The second pinch was held down towards the Mother Earth and placed within the bowl. Next beginning with the Power of the East she included a pinch for the Powers of the East, South, West, and North. In an earlier discussion she had compared this concept of a Power in each direction to Christian Archangels, to the Lords of the Watchtowers or the Ancient Ones of the Pagan traditions. She then offered a pinch to all the Grandfathers and then the Grandfather of the region, whom she invited to smoke with us. She related a Grandfather would be the equivalent of a Hindu deva or a

Christian angel. She offered a pinch to Grandfather Eagle and to the individual spirit-eagle she worked with. She gave thanks for guidance and blessings and asked for their protection while we smoked. She filled the rest of her pipe with the mineral, vegetable, animal, and human kingdoms, and for those who had passed on, then she joined the pipe bowl and pipe stem together which represented the harmony and union of all seeming duality, the contents of the bowl represented the inter-relatedness of all Life. She was praying for everything, with everything.

Eve began the smoking of the pipe by touching the bowl to the floor (symbolically the Earth) and lighting the pipe. She then lifted it with the pipe stem towards the sky drew a clockwise circle and said, "Grandfather Eagle, I send a voice for all the prayers in this pipe, and for protection and thanksgiving. She then prayed for my healing and for Ruth and Peggy. She then lowered the pipe and began smoking. Eve smoked as she instructed us to, directing the first exhalation to the Great Spirit, the next downwards to the Mother Earth, then beginning in the east to the four directions. At that point she told us you were to pray for those you knew in need and for yourself, and for the Earth as a whole. Eve prayed in silence with her eyes closed, blowing smoke out directly in front of her. Minutes passed as she smoked, seeming deep in contemplation. Then one by one as she obviously but silently prayed for each of us she blew the smoke of her exhalation out covering each of us in the smoke. After doing this individually to all three of us she smoked again with her attention in prayer and her exhalations undirected. The pipe was then passed clockwise around the circle each of us smoking towards the six directions and then for ourselves as directed. When the pipe got back to Eve she finished smoking it she rested the pipe briefly on her knees and then raised it the extent of her arms and said, "We offer and present to

You ourselves, all that we are and all that we will be when we go shining. Uniting with the blessed company of all faithful creatures throughout the worlds that You have made, and all these here present, we say yes, yes, yes, yes to Your divine will for us and all that you have created. Then she lowered the pipe to her knees and continued" "We sit here in Your Holy Presence. We know that You are everywhere and in all that You have made. Of ourselves we can do nothing, but with Your Indwelling Presence all things are possible. We know that we can have those things for which we ask aright."

Eve lifted the pipe slightly and changed her plural reference to singular, "I ask for the prayers in this pipe, for those whom I remember and those whom I forget, for all who have smoked this pipe with me and those who can be reached through this pipe for a blessing, may they all go shining. We pray for our friends, our relatives, our loved ones, and for those who have taken off their overcoats (died), may they all go shining.

We thank You for creating us and for these paths You have placed us on. May we travel straight and true and shining towards You. We thank You for the interdependence of all created things, that we are all in You, and You in all of us. We thank You for everything. Amen."

Our visit concluded with a warm good-by and an invitation to visit her again. Eve told Peggy and me to work together every morning or night in healing and prayer and to come back for more instruction. She added that those who seek help from a pipe healer should bring tobacco with them as an offering and present it to the healer as a preliminary to the healing work.

In two weeks my girlfriend Peggy and I returned brining with us my brother and his girlfriend who were both in our group and interested in Native American practices. Ruth was unable to join us so the four of us rode from Atlanta up into the mountains on a beautiful, bright, clear autumn day. On the way up we found a very recent road kill which turned out to be a Red-shouldered Hawk. It was a magnificent bird with very little damage except where its neck had been broken. We said a prayer for its spirit as we thought appropriate and then took the feathers and claws, reverently burying the remains. This may sound barbaric but for those who value the qualities of such feathers there is no more humanitarian way to acquire them.

Upon our arrival and after the customary introductions we made a present of our tobacco and the prettiest and largest of the hawk feathers. To our surprise Eve related that in the tradition she practiced all birds of prey were referred to as eagles. Even the often maligned crow in her tradition was referred to as the little black eagle. Her own spirit eagle it turned out was what she referred to as a red shouldered "eagle." She told us how, as I was later to witness myself, that birds would often circle overhead as she smoked her pipe, among the most regular and visible would be a Red-shouldered Hawk. This substitutionary use of the term eagle was something I had never read or heard of before. In fact it was to be some eight years later before I heard it explained again in almost identical terms on Paiute land before a Sweat Lodge. Of course there are tribal variations but the eagle is sacred because it flies higher than any other bird, being closest to the Great Spirit it serves as his emissary. Since all birds of prey fly and exhibit the strength of the predator they all share the qualities of the eagle. My understanding of this concept still lacks clarity because of the inclusion of the crow and a lack of reference to other "scavenger" birds such as the buzzard. The owl doesn't seem to qualify being considered in Paiute mythology to be the harbinger of bad news or death.

It was obvious to us that Eve was genuinely happy with our gift and we felt warmly received. The visit went through much the same process as the earlier visit. The discussions were centered on personal experiences and spiritual understanding, ours as well as hers. The Native American beliefs and practices were the focus of much her attention, but the healing system she taught us was of a more eclectic nature.

Eve taught us this healing method and told us to teach it to others who could utilize it. She stressed that not all people could come by sacred healing tools, not all people needed them and even those that owned them might not have them ready during a time of need. I took written notes during our discussion and will try to relate the basics of that system.

"The Great Spirit, the Mother Father Creator of all Life, is within all, is the source of all; is the sustainer of all. The Great Spirit is a unity, a harmony within itself, and is in, as well as beyond the duality with which it created material reality. As the atom consists of an electron which is negative, a proton which is positive, and the neutral neutron so does the Great Spirit exist throughout the duality of material existence. All humans have a potentially self-conscious and divine spark of this Great Spirit inherent in the constitution of the soul and spirit of man. Although this potential exists; it is only through life in the dualistic material world that the soul and spirit can attain the experience and wisdom, i.e. growing, that the human consciousness needs to manifest that potential. The individual can aid this process by offering themselves in service to the Great Spirit."

"I came to understand this as a child when one day in my imagination I pictured God as a toymaker sitting at his table filled with the toys He had made. His toys were his children, they were humanity and they had free will. I realized that if one of the toys presented itself with a rusty part in need of replacement surely the toymaker would gladly repair it. The Great Spirit loves all of Its children and when you turn to the Creator for help such help will be given."

"All religions around the world use the concept and symbol of light when referring to beneficent forces or higher spiritual realities. This light often has either one of two meanings. In the physical reality of duality and the senses this light is the chi of the Taoist, the Prana of the Hindu, the Mana of the Polynesian, the Aeither of the ancient Greeks, and the Akasha of the modern occultist. Anyone can increase their supply of this simply by deep breathing. I have found and recommend a pattern of 3:3:3 to be effective. While relaxed and comfortable, with the back straight, inhale for a count of three, hold for a count of three, exhale for a count of three and pause. During that pause don't count or think, try to be perfectly still, at peace, empty. As you continue, your breathing will become slower and deeper, it is the evenness of the rhythm which is important."

This is one kind of light and is basic. The Light of the world's religions is a higher concept referring symbolically to the Wisdom, Beauty, and Love of divinity; or to the sensations experienced by the beholder of divinity. This Light seen by the mystics of all ages is not just symbolic but is in itself a reality and manifestation of the divine. This healing system is based around the premise that if you offer yourself in service as a clear and open channel that this Light - this Great White Light - this healing energy will flow through you to the person or people in need. This is done through prayer and by using your imagination. You pray that you will be a clear and open channel and that your patient(s) will receive healing as is best for them. Next you open your passive side palm parallel with the ground.

You point your active side hand towards the patient. Now it doesn't matter about left and right, everyone except the absolutely ambidextrous know immediately which is which. In your imagination you picture a column of Light pouring down from the sky. You may picture it pouring down around you and forming a cone of Light or you may picture it in a column pouring down into your open passive palm and pouring out of your active hand into your patient to heal them. Whether you see it come only into your palm or see a cone of Light you sill imagine Light coming into one hand and pouring out the other. Now as you get more accomplished in the system you will develop sensations that function as a feedback system to let you know you're succeeding. When you begin and you have no confirmatory sensations or visions do not be alarmed. If you call out for help; help will be given. The important part is to offer yourself as an open channel and to call for help. Whether or not you feel such sensations or not has no limiting effect on the healing.

These feedback sensations will vary among individuals and the same individual may experience different sensations over time. These sensations may be in the form of discernible heat, or a feeling of pressure, or the sensation of a breeze flowing around your palm and fingers. You may have no sensations and yet see the entire process in your mind's eye. You will learn to trust your intuition as to the length of a treatment but in the beginning always work as a channel until in your imagination the patient is surrounded by, filled up with, and virtually overflowing with vibrant white Light. This Light is the same Light that pours from the sacred healing objects. Do not be misled by the simplicity of this system for it is highly effective."

Eve went about things on our second visit much as she had on the first, introductions, conversation, smudging, healing, and then smoking the sacred pipe. She did healing on all of us, although she worked a much longer time on me. Her techniques were the same, the difference being that for the others she was cleaning out their auras and beefing up their energy fields whereas with me she went through her complete healing procedure. She probably worked on them from three to five minutes, and on me for fifteen to twenty-five minutes.

Because there is a sensual-sensory aspect to participation in mystical and ritual activity I must comment on my feelings and sensations while Eve performed her healing work on me. My experience could be equated with that of a light and pleasant meditation. I did not experience a heat, pressure, or breeze. I did not see light, colors, or undergo any rapid or extreme alteration in consciousness. I felt calm, relaxed, and experienced a generalized feeling of well-being.

The others reported a similar lack of exotic sensations but did experience the calm and feeling of well-being. These experiences were noted and reflected on but were not so strong or special to either confirm or contract from her teachings.

After the healing we went outside to smoke the sacred pipe. Her procedure was the same as before; she smudged everything, put the pipe together, prayed as she filled it, smoked and exhaled on us one by one as she went clockwise around the circle. Then she passed the pipe clockwise, each of us smoked and passed the pipe clockwise, she finished and said her closing prayers. She also blessed the different feathers and pieces of jewelry we handed her by smudging them and praying silently while holding them.

As we got ready to go she told us that she was really glad to have met us and addressed us in a general way if we were ever in California to visit her. She then turned to me and said that if I came to visit she would teach me as her student and introduce me to her medicine man. She said she couldn't promise anything, but when I met him I could ask him for a four day healing sweat lodge. She again reiterated that she could not speak for him, but that she would do for me what she could on my behalf and that it was a very powerful healing ritual.

The car ride back to Atlanta was filled with conversation about Eve, her practices, and her world view. On an emotional level we concurred that there was warmth and sincerity in what Eve said and did that was easy to respond to. Although we had gone to visit and learn she had drawn each of us out in conversation and we had parted feeling as though in a scant space of a few hours she really had gotten to know us and we her. She did not charge for her services as a healer other than the ritual gift of tobacco so her motives were certainly not monetary or that I could see, even self-serving from a mainstream point of view. Because of her credibility - the fact that she had authored books and taught creative writing at various colleges and her sheer command of her subject matter - had relaxed all apprehension that she might be a member of the "lunatic fringe" so attracted to anything mysterious or exotic. Having been the recipient of the healing treatment, effectiveness aside, I had to appreciate anyone spending that much time and concentration devoted to improving my health.

We compared our understandings of what she had said in an attempt to summarize what we could of her world view. We did this in our on terms and not necessarily in hers although our attempt was to reconstruct what she had taught. I had my notes to refer to, which aided our recollection. Although my brother and I had smoked a sacred pipe once before meeting Eve, I would say none of us had any previous in depth exposure to Native American practices. We shared common exposure to such books as those about medicine men like Black Elk and Rolling Thunder, to books by Calos Casteneda, to classics like <u>Bury My Heart At Wounded Knee</u> by Dee Brown and Hymeyohsts Storm's <u>Seven Arrows.</u> We all knew that seeing Rolling Thunder in a Billy Jack movie was not much background but there was an implicitly to it which did not make an in depth background necessary. For the sake of simplicity I will summarize our understanding.

"Man and the reality he lives in is multi—dimensional. Man in his many aspects exists in many worlds simultaneously. All that exist is somewhere on a chain of evolution, with the Great Spirit as the original source and the final goal. From the healers' point of view everything from the sun and moon, to people, to a tree, to a rock, everything is alive. Although the Hindu says there are seven planes of existence, and the

Kabbalah teaches that there are ten interpenetrating worlds, these are only vague road maps and there are no limitations.

In relation to man and the reality we live in everything you encounter can be understood to have some sort of existence on at least three levels. The first is physical, everything that is has, an energy basis, has Life Force, has Chi, and has an electromagnetic field. Every planet, plant, and person has a force field. The human force field is circular and of various sizes emanating from the radius of the solar plexus. Likewise everything, everything has an existence that in some way corresponds to our emotional-mental complex. This is the human soul, and the Earth has a soul, so does a tree, and in some form, so does a rock. Mystics of all ages have observed this aspect of humanity and referred to it as the aura. High thoughts and positive emotions are said to emanate beautiful colors whereas disease shows up as holes, and dark spots. Thoughts and emotions are a form of directed energy and when concentrated are creative and causal. The human aura varies in size, is oval shaped, and emanates from the heart. It is from this aspect of his being that man can project his consciousness, travel in his astral body, communicate with spirits, and participate in the constant war between the forces of health and Life against the forces of Death, disease, and dissolution. It is this part of our being which is growing and evolving towards spiritual self-consciousness by participating in the harsh realities of physical existence, this world rightly called by some the land of the adversary.

The Great Spirit is in all things and all things are in the Great Spirit. The closest our human understanding came close to this Great Spirit is love. Why this Divine Love, and Divine Unity would take some of Itself and divide it into the positive and negative forces that give rise to the involutions and evolutions of Spirit to matter and matter to Spirit of the various chains of evolving life is a mystery. The mystery schools of Greece and Rome, like the practices of the Native shaman aim at the understanding and solution of such mysteries through an initiatory progression.

The purpose of this initiatory process is for the soul to come into conscious union with the spirit. Little is understood of the energy basis or force field of the human spirit. The best understanding of the human spirit comes from the image of The Great Spirit in manifestation as Godhead, as the central Spiritual Sun, of which each human spirit is a divine spark. Each human being at the most original and basic level is a spark of this divine fire, and the aware, self-conscious identification with this divine spark is every human's ultimate goal. Taoist tradition holds that one "breath" of this divine fire can make what is dead and rotting new and whole again.

There were certain practices Eve recommended such as talking directly to the Great Spirit as though to a close friend. When sick she advised that you talk directly of the cells and molecules asking them to cooperate. She taught that help was always available because the Great Spirit loves all of Its creations. The energy form of this help would be in the white light of healing, the golden light of divine wisdom, the rose red light of divine love. Although we pray to the Mother-Father Creator of all Life the help we receive comes from the source through some intermediary agency. Whether this agency is called a Power of the East or Grandfather Buffalo or Mother Earth there is a spirit, an angel, some agency in between. In the Holy Bible a warning is issued; that no man shall see the face of God and live.

As the healer is channel of energy into the patient, so is the angel a channel of energy to the healer. Eve associated the Power of the East with Light and the source of Light. The Power of the South is associated with warm and healing winds, the West with justice and balance, the North with cold and purifying winds.

Eve taught that our true nature was spiritual and that our bodies were like overcoats we wore while incarnate. She said we should enjoy all things and be good guest. Those without pipes can meditate with candles casting all their dross and impurities into the flame.

In such things the color of the candle is important because colors have an influence of their own. Her associations of colors to their qualities and influences are:

- Red- life force, energy,

- Orange- the sun

- Purple- A spiritual color for understanding and relief from sorrow

- Green- a color of nature, for accomplishing goals

- Blue- light is devotion, dark is for occult development

- White- purification and healing..

These influences can be utilized by mentally visualizing the color, meditating with that color candle, or drinking water from glass containers of that color after a few hours exposure to the sun. She cautioned not to be overly burdened by a science oriented rationalism but to work from the heart.

She stressed a life of service and participation in the conflict that was real and unresolved except at the "highest, deepest, and most unified" aspect of the Mother-Father Creator of All Life. The risk to body and soul of participating in this conflict are undertaken for the reward and satisfaction of the service and expected enhancement of individual understanding, power, and love.

The Circle is a Symbol of Life

Eve used the circle as a prominent symbol in many ways. She said that the Creator began manifest reality with a clockwise circle; that the Sea of Chaos, the Womb of Space would be outside that circle and manifest reality within. In the war between what Eve called the Army of Darkness against the Army of Light, the circle was a primary tool of protection and psychic self-defense. This was done by drawing a clockwise circle of White Light in one's imagination, at chest height, with a radius about arm's length.

She used the symbol of the circle to explain away the seeming conflicts between the various religions and occult traditions of the world saying that on the circumference of the circle what may seem to stand in a direct 180° contradiction will find harmony and union at center of the circle, where dwells the heart of all true religion, which is Truth and Love.

When comparing American Indian symbology with the symbols used by other Nature-dependent pre-Industrial societies of the past, and present, and various western esoteric philosophies we find the circle and the cross used recurrently, often with a surprising similarity in meaning.

The Great Spirit, God, sometimes Divine Will is often symbolized by a plain circle or a circle with a dot at the center.

The Great Spirit

God

Divine Will

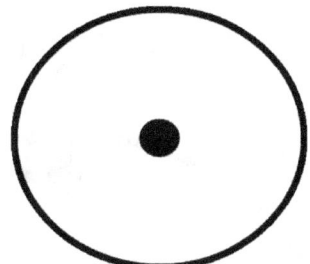

Mother Earth or life on Earth is often symbolized by the equidistant cross within the circle. The arms of the cross represent the four universal elements of Life, which come together on planet Earth and in the human experience

Mother Earth

The four elements were often symbolically associated with the four directions. In the northern hemisphere, their most common representations were air-mental-east, fire-spiritual-south, water-emotional-west, and earth-physical-north.

Earth- North- Physical

Water- West- Emotional

Air- East- Mental

Fire- South- Spiritual

The four elements have their correspondences in Jung's psychology.

He lists the four functions of the psyche as sensation, thinking intuition, and feeling.

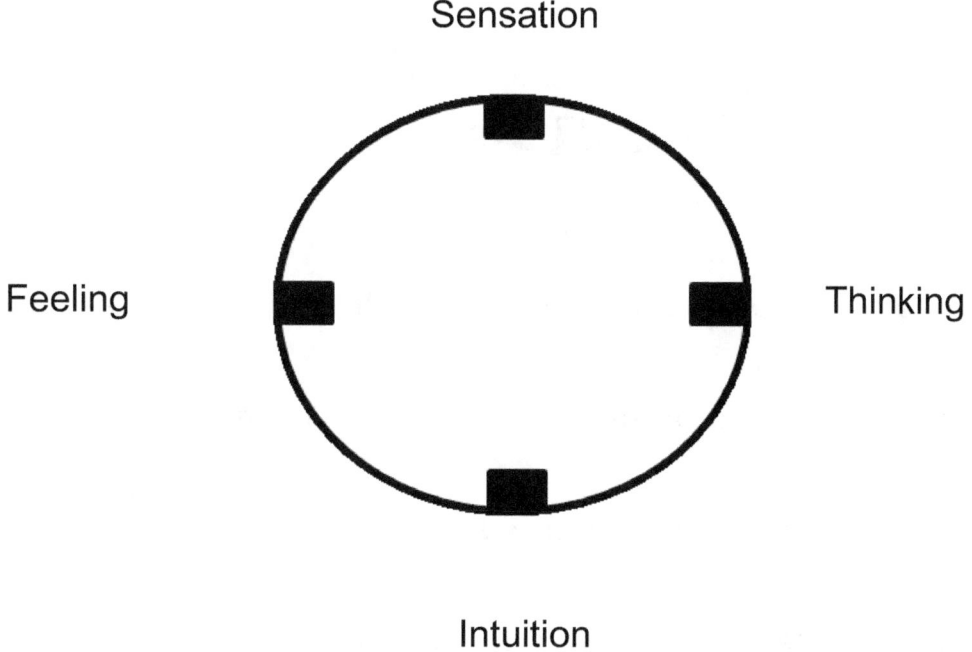

Since our religious traditions tell us our world was created by Divinity and that humanity was created in the image of divinity.

The four elements of Classical Greece, Rome, of Ancient Egypt and India, and the Holy Bible were and still are often symbolized by the circle divided in four right angles.

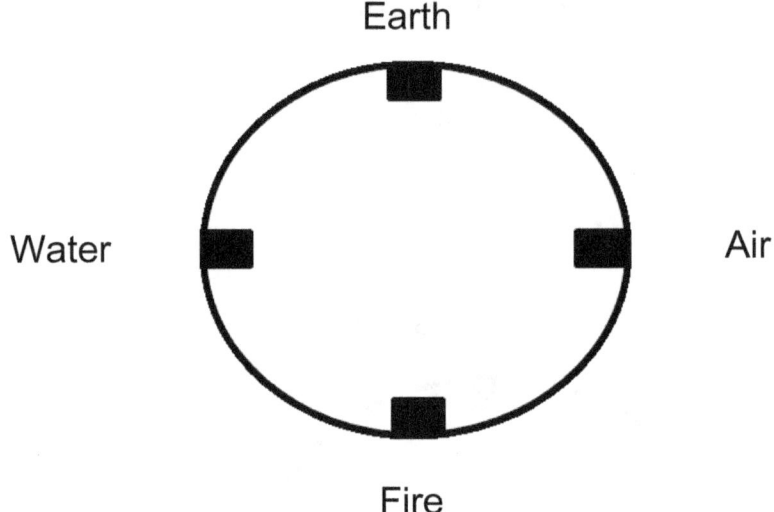

The theologies and cosmologies of the ancient, classical, and biblical worlds were based on the four elements. Today's periodic table of elements contains well over a hundred elements, but in the past reality consisted of four elements or worlds. These four elements were not thought of as purely physical, but represented spiritual aspects of life as well.

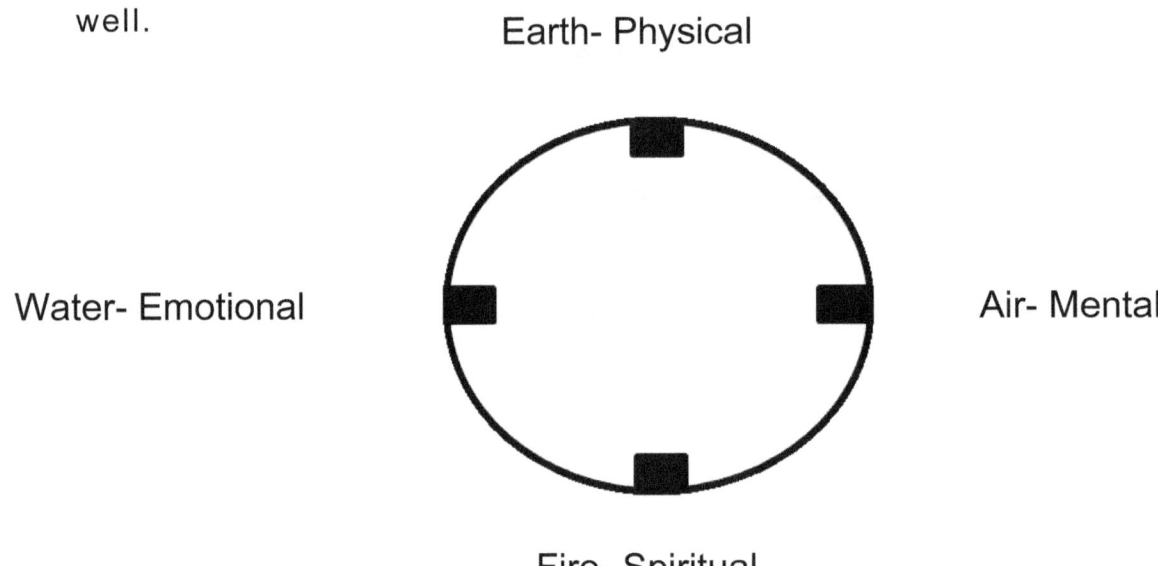

Divinity also can be symbolized by the circle. The bible says God's name is I AM THAT I AM, and God is described as Light, Love, and Spirit.

In the pre-Christian European traditions the element fire is sometimes divided into two aspects. The physical element fire is thought of as symbolizing human will or life-force, and the element Spirit or Aether symbolizes the non-physical higher spiritual aspects of life. In such symbology, the four worlds or elements are subordinate to Spirit.

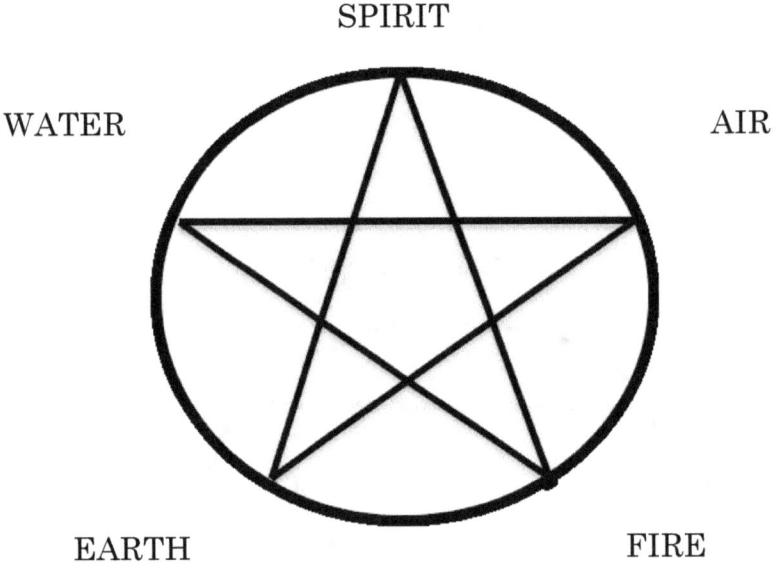

The cross as a symbol pre-dates Christianity, and like the circle was used in almost every part of the world. It wasn't until Constantine in the early 300's that the cross was used as a Christian cross represents the scheme of four elements, with fire (spirit) dominant over the other three elements of being.

SPIRIT - FIRE

WATER　　　　　AIR

EARTH

Eve Eaton wrote about the similarity in American Indian and Christian cosmologies. The Indian have a Creator and four creative forces-powers-elements. She explains that the Great Spirit, as Creator, is the Thunderbird and the four creative forces are the Grandfathers of the four directions.

She said Christianity also had a creator and four creative forces. She saw the Creator as the word, the logos, and the four creative forces symbolized in Revelations and in Ezekiel. In Ezekiel 1:5-28, Ezekiel describes four creatures, each having four faces, and four wings, and the attributes of a calf, an angel (face of a man), a lion, and an eagle. In Revelations 4:6-8, John describes four beasts before the throne of God, again, a calf, an angel (face of a man), a lion, and an eagle.

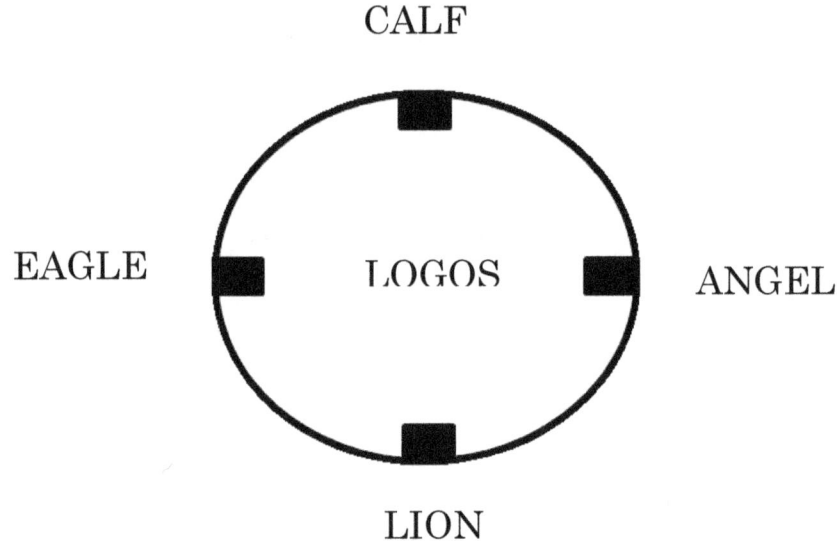

In astrology of Classical Greece and Rome, as well as modern astrology, the four elements are fundamental, and the biblical symbols are repeated in the four fixed signs of Aquarius, Leo, Scorpio, and Taurus.

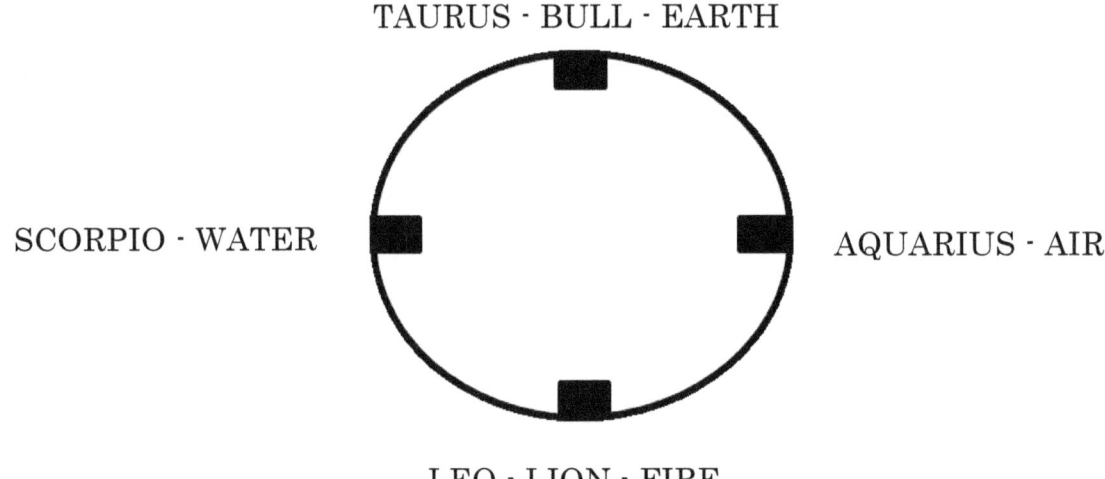

Circles are also used to symbolize the cycles of the natural world and human life.

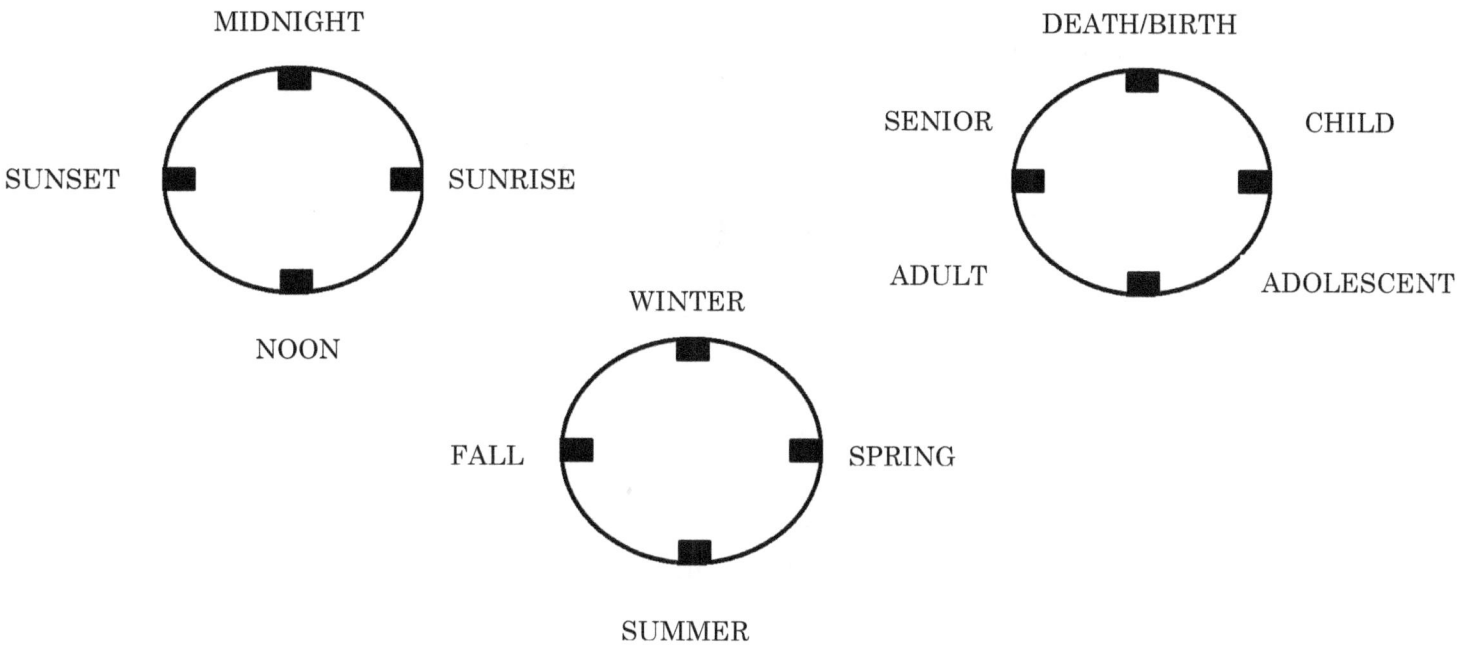

The circle divided into eights, the wheel with eight spokes, is a symbol found in Hinduism, Buddhism, and in pre-Christian Europe, where it was represented the wheel of the sun, the wheel of the year, the witch's wheel. The eight pagan holidays were a combination of the lunar agrarian year and festivals, with the solar year, the equinoxes and solstices.

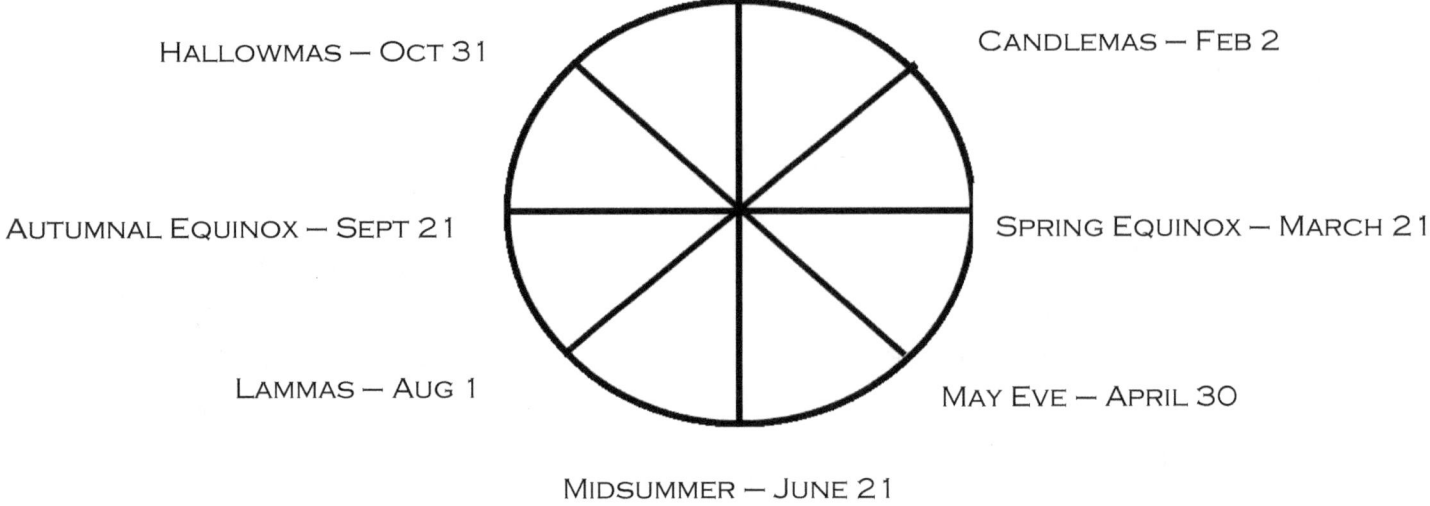

In our discussions with Eve, we dwelled mainly on the Native American beliefs but our conversations did touch the topic of Christianity. Ruth and Eve as do many people who might refer to themselves as Esoteric Christians, would explain their understanding that what is referred to as Christ is a universal principle of Love that animated the man known as Jesus from his Baptism and the descent of the dove, until his crucifixion, at which point he cries out "why hast Thou forsaken me." Eve and Ruth also seemed to indicate that the man Jesus, who for three years was overshadowed by this universal principle of love, was the first perfected being in the human evolutionary chain of reincarnation. Jesus as perfected man was capable of letting this universal principle and spirit of love teach and speak through him. Thus in their minds there is an association, if not equation of: That Aspect of the Creator Which Is Love = Universal Love = Christ = the Christ Light (in our solar system, at least).

Eve was rare and unique in my experience in that she had found a harmonious synthesis between the religious systems native to North America with those of Pre-Christian Europe, the great religions of the East, and an esoteric Christianity. It seemed to me then, and still does, that she had done something that many desire to do, whether they are consciously cognizant of it or not. She had attained an understanding and ability to functionally utilize the various and diverse traditions of her ancestral and cultural heritage.

Eve and I shared a few characteristics in common, which may have been part of the reason she became my teacher and my friend. She had written poetry since her youth and so had I. She was proud of her English heritage as I was my Scott-Irish, but she was especially glad to have blood - which linked her to the continent she lived on, and the tradition she practiced. She had a small amount of Native ancestry she referred to at that time as Algonquin. My grandfather's grandmother was full Cherokee, and my grandmother's heritage is part Creek Indian. I likewise was happy to be linked by blood to the continent I lived on. The spiritual heritage of my ancestors as well as hers, before Christianization, is that of Nature reverence and Nature worship, as practiced by the Druids, the Wicca, and the Native Americans. She and I shared a deep love of Nature. This awe and love of Nature is not Semitic or scripturally Christian, and almost stands in opposition to the dominion Jehovah patriarically grants man over Nature and its inhabitants. Yet the Universal Love and mercy symbolized by Jesus Christ is such an incredibly dominant and powerful symbol to those raised in a Christian setting it cannot be forgotten or ignored but must be meaningfully accepted, synthesized, or denied. She had attained a synthesis that I and other young people found interesting and somewhat novel. She managed to retain Nature reverence and retain a belief in the Love of Christ as a universal principle within Nature – the Christ Light. She accepted that the nature of this universal love was exhibited in the life of Jesus. That Eve and I were of the inclination to write poetry, revere Nature, and explore spiritual realities was more than enough in common to overcome any obstacles created by our age difference of half a century. I resolved on that second ride back from the mountains to go visit Eve, to meet her medicine man, and to ask for the four day sweat.

Encouragement in this resolve came from two sources. Ruth reminded me of what she referred to as an old occult axiom, "When the student is ready, the master appears," and advised me to accept Eve as my spiritual teacher. I had arranged for my lawyer, Joe Harmon, to meet Eve. Besides being a nationally renowned trial lawyer he was a deeply spiritual man, conversant with Hinduism and deeply committed to the teachings of Meher Baba. When he came back from meeting Eve; he also encouraged me to accept Eve as my teacher. Joe and I had spent long hours in conversation and we had come to understand something of each other's beliefs, and though we didn't always see things the same, we shared a mutual respect and loving tolerance. His comment was that "Eve is uniquely you." Both Joe and Ruth reported that Eve had enjoyed our visits and had warm feelings for us.

It would be a year before I was able to go visit Eve. During this time, we were in contact by phone and letter, and I attempted to implement her teachings in my life. Although my relationship with Peggy was dissolving in all realms but spiritual, we continued to work as Eve instructed. This mainly took the form of a daily healing meditation involving smudging, praying, and attempting to channel the healing white Light to each other and those we knew in need.

During this year I have records of six public healings I performed utilizing Eve's techniques. By public I mean that it was not Peggy and I working on each other, but a healing requested by Ruth or someone in our group. This request came either directly or secondarily from someone who knew about Eve, that she had instructed me and blessed my healing feather and my healing stone. These healings were not in lieu of medical help but sought to relieve pain and quicken the healing process. The symptoms treated ranged from a broken arm, to an ovarian cyst, to simple tooth ache. It would be impossible to determine to what extent healing might be quickened in such situations, but all patients experienced an immediate reduction or ceasing of pain, at least temporarily. As someone trained in hypnosis, the removal of pain through such strong suggestions as those related verbally in prayer or non-verbally through use of the stone and feather is neither miraculous nor surprising. To the patient in pain, the removal of pain is a wonderful event, however interpreted.

To the novice healer six successful reductions or eliminations of pain was certainly more encouraging than if nothing had happened, and I knew that Eve would be pleased that I was implementing her teachings. I also knew that Ruth would pass on a good report to Eve, and that could only make things better when I arrived in California.

Arriving

I began my journey to visit Eve in the autumn of 1977. I drove up from Atlanta during the height of the fall season, awed by the dazzlingly rich reds and golds which are the hallmark of the southern fall. My Volvo made it as far as Bowling Green, Kentucky before making a convincing statement in favor of American cars. I finally made it to California by hitchhiking down to Nashville and flying on to San Francisco,

I rented a car there and arrived to visit Eve during the last days of October. Eve was expecting me and I was housed in Edie's house which shared adjacent backyards with Eve's. Edie was Eve's right hand, her close friend and co-worker, and in no time flat she was my "mother" in California.

My relationship with Eve also was immediately deepened and she became my "grandmother" in both senses as an older woman who is loved and respected, who feels like and is treated like family and in the

Indian way, as a respected elder and teacher, an older woman of authority.

That these women were used to visitors was immediately apparent, and besides the space I occupied at Edie's they had a large recreational vehicle which could sleep two, and there was a government maintained camping facility nearby. Edie related to me that the calls for Eve as a healer and as a speaker had been continually increasing. Edie was fifteen of twenty years younger than Eve, a handsome blond woman who was experienced in the administration of artist's communities. She was helping Eve operate the non-profit corporation Eve had started in order to accomplish various spiritual and artistic goals. The corporation, Draco, supported local arts, helped Eve publish and disseminate her work, and to record and distribute the work of Eve's friend classical pianist Iren Marrik. This "corporation" was housed, of course, in Edie's house and the one Eve shared with Iren.

I found myself a young man of the sixties and seventies surrounded by three unique women, each possessing a strong and independent character, involved in a fascinating array of activities. The one thing I found that these three women had in common was their strong dislike for rock and roll. Although they liked some of what my generation had done they agreed that we were too wild, too promiscuous, and that the music we liked was bad for humans, plants, and other living things. I can remember sitting with my grandmother as a child, before she passed on, when out of love I would sit there with her and endure the Lawrence Welk Show - wondering how anyone could like it, and realizing the vast difference of taste between generations. So I sat there and smiled and told them I liked classical and rock, and limited my radio listening to those times I was driving alone.

Although I was not without curiosity about the personal histories of these three women, it was not my place to ask personal questions.

Through the course of normal conversation I discovered that Eve and Edie both had grown children whose fathers had passed on. Iren was born into Hungarian aristocracy and a lifestyle now extinct. She told me stories that as a child she had watched the servants clean their grand ballroom by attaching mops to their feet and skating around the massive hall. I found out to my pleasure and delight that she was also a gourmet chef. Iren, unlike Edie, was not involved in Eve's spiritual work. Eve and Iren were friends who shared a love of music and the arts, and they had both experienced as contemporaries a world that has passed and will never be again, a world that was innocent of the world wars to come and the technology of global destruction that was their legacy. To hear these two talk about Europe before, during, and after World War I was an educational experience. Because Iren was not involved in the spiritual work, she would openly enjoy her drink and her cigarette, and she loved a good joke. Her love of life was my kind of hedonism, but as I will explain shortly my spiritual pursuits were going to cost much more than missing a few hours of my favorite music.

As I came to decipher the individual elements out of the array of activities I began to understand the roles and responsibilities of the core members of my new extended family. Eve was the inward spiritual powerhouse and the outward spokesman. Her job was to heal and help, as a healer, lecturer, and as a bridge between the ancient wisdom of the Native Americans and those modern Americans who felt themselves to be spiritually bankrupt. She was a mystic with a vision, that her work and the work of many others would help to elevate the consciousness of enough people so that the extreme pollution of the Earth our Mother would be stopped and cleansed.

Edie's job was to handle the logistics of the trips and the appearances and to keep things going on the daily basis and to deal with the frequent and numerous visitors such as myself. As I mentioned earlier she helped with the paper work and correspondences of Draco, and she also put out the Draco newsletter. Edie was Eves' majordomo, and on her shoulders fell the driving, the management of Draco sponsored concerts; and a thousand other miscellaneous task. Among these was to make sure that the over enthusiastic didn't monopolize Eve's time, so that she could maintain a good work rate on the book she was writing.

Iren's work was her piano, and she performed in the concerts Draco would sponsor and record. In a conversation with a musicologist visiting from New York who'd come to interview Iren and hear her play; I was told that there were only two people still living that had received the classical training Iren had, and that she was the only one who could still play with great beauty.

I was often amazed at the number and constancy of the flow of people. There were the relatives of the three women, their friends; many of whom were interesting writers or musicians; those who came to interview or study, and those who came to be healed. It was a stimulating environment to be in, rich in diversity and one that would keep the visitor mentally keen.

Besides Eve's work as a poet, author, pipe woman and healer, she was involved in three areas of group activity. The first of these I will mention probably consumed the least of her time while I was present, but that is no indication of what it meant to her. I can say very little about it; I know that there was a Co-Masonic lodge and that she was involved - I would imagine as the leader or highest degree initiate: When I asked her about it, she showed me some books, and talked to me about it, but that was enough to satisfy my interest and was as close to any involvement as I ever got. I imagine that their lodge met once or twice a month, but I don't know any specifics.

On Friday nights an eclectic study group would meet at Edie's house and Eve would lead in prayer, meditation and discussion. They would all read the same book and discuss it, and sometimes they would have pot-luck dinners. One book that they used quite often was also one of Ruth's favorite, Mary Strong's *Letters of the Scattered Brotherhood*. Most of these people were white, fellow town's people of various ages. Some were active in the Co-Masons, a few of the young ones and Edie went to the sweats and knew of Eve's full involvement with the Indians. Most of the town's people knew little or nothing about the sweat lodge or Eve's involvement, and it was kept that way. So in the discussion groups Eve drew from her wide range of knowledge, and although she did not ignore the Indian spiritual tradition, it was not the central focus.

The third group activity was the sweat lodge and other ceremonies of what Eve would call the Indian way, by which she meant the traditional practices and beliefs. Although I had come to study under and be worked on by Eve, one of her reasons for wanting me to come and one of the reasons I had made the long journey was the probability that I would be allowed into the sweat lodge. Eve wasted no time in facilitating this. Although the primary activities relevant to this paper were those of smoking the sacred pipe with Eve, undergoing healing from Eve, and our mutual participation in the sweats; our relationship as student-teacher was of a more eclectic nature. Eve and I shared a great love for the Earth Mother and were both interested in the Mystery Schools of the ancient world.

We discussed the work of the group in Atlanta and she reviewed the rituals involved and she made suggestions. I was deeply interested in mysteries pertaining to the Earth Mother and the World Mother, more specifically the mysteries pertaining to the Virgin Goddess and the mysteries of Isis. I have been told that the secret ancient wisdom of the Hebrews is called the Kabala, a term derived from the letters Q-B-L, meaning mouth-to-ear. This is the manner in which I was instructed, in the manner of a higher initiate to a lower initiate, never to be written, never to be spoken of except to another initiate. My experience with the Indians had an equally severe injunction. I promised Eve, as she requested, that I would never reveal the real names of Medicine Men or any real location, or any information about ritual that could be replicated, except to those she approved or in a really special case, those that my discernment instructed me to. There were many reasons for this, legal, cultural, social, and others I may still be unaware of, so I agreed then. However, once ritual has been divulged by others, the oath is not binding. I say this in the same manner that she related it to me. Although I can't reveal new information, there is very little that Black Elk didn't already reveal in *The Sacred Pipe* about the ritual of the sweat lodge.

Besides the injunctions of silence there were other changes that I accepted when I arrived. One that was drastic, but primarily unconscious was the modification of my daily speech patterns. The more colorful phrases of my daily language had been picked up on various construction and demolition jobs and were not apropos to my new surroundings or the company of older and cultured women. Edie explained that since I was there for healing, and that what you eat is what your body has to work with, I should eat a good balanced diet. She saw to this, except for those exquisite moments of debauchery when Edie was away and Iren would bring over some incredibly rich gourmet delight. This, of course, was all too rare. My regular diet was also supplied by a good dose of vitamins and enzymes to aid in the full and proper digestion of food. I did not then, and am not sure now if those first few days and weeks were a period of probation and testing. Eve told me simply that the right question would earn the right answer, and that while I was there seeking her knowledge and aid I would not indulge in the consumption of alcoholic beverages, marijuana, or any other drugs, period. It was not stated in the form of a question or a polite request, I was there for her help, and those were the terms.

None of this was very surprising, except the emphasis on secrecy about names and locations, which seemed to be in contradiction to the example set by Eve herself, in her first book about her Paiute experiences. Then I found out that it was because of negative Paiute reaction to the openness of her book that she was now so emphatic about secrecy. Although Eve had dedicated the book to the Paiutes of her valley, whom she referred to as a proud and patient people, from their perspective, she had made several mistakes.

As I attempted to understand this antagonism towards her book I realized that to grasp the whole picture I would have to examine it from several different levels of magnification, from the larger national picture, to the smaller specific local picture. *The Snowy Earth Comes Gliding* was published in 1974, during a time when the Native Americans were reasserting themselves politically on a national level. This was happening in many ways. From inside the legal and political system Indians sought, and on occasion received, some of what they had been promised in treaties at the times of their military defeats. In 1973 there was the much publicized take-over at Wounded Knee. On the Pine Ridge Oglala Lakota reservation there was a civil war between the supporters of AIM – the American Indian Movement and Tribal leader Dick Wilson's private army, The GOON's – the heavily armed Guards of the Oglala Nation, backed up by armed agents of the Bureau of Indian Affairs and the FBI. There was a 1975 firefight resulting in the death of two FBI agents, a very questionable 1977 trial, and the highly controversial incarceration of Leonard Peltier. Amnesty International, among many other groups, has called the trial highly questionable; there was apparently massive and illegal coercion of prosecution witnesses by the BIA and FBI. One critic claimed that every single prosecution witness was a victim of this coercion and later recanted their testimony. The Val

Kilmer movie *Thunderheart* is Hollywood's take on the Pine Ridge situation at that time.

Political groups such as the militant American Indian Movement proclaimed that the Indians were the spiritual guardians and caretakers of the entire Planet Earth, and especially this land, this continent they know as Turtle Island. Several Medicine Men publicly confirmed this idea, which was just a part of the resurgence of a great pride in their traditional identity.

This was a time of Indian revival, but certainly not one of total victory. There was and still remains a great gap of understanding between the cultures in conflict. Very few of those mythical normal Americans watching the nightly news understood that gap when they watched scenes from the uprising at Wounded Knee. So few understood the cultural scars of military defeat, the historical attempt of one culture to debase another, the generations of Indian children taken away from their parents and relatives, and sent off to boarding schools where they were beaten for speaking their native language. With such gaps in understanding it is easy to imagine that while making progress, Native Americans were not quick to trust a culture that for centuries, since the first contact, has used, killed, chained, or corralled them

Snowy Earth and a Spiritual Hierarchy

A short review of Eve's book will shed light on this situation. It is filled with photographs and verse from poems and songs. On the back Eve is introduced and the biography there is worthy of summation.

She is introduced as a writer born of Canadian parents, educated in Canada, England, and France, residing in the U.S. since W.W.II. She is credited with twenty novels, three collections of poetry, and twenty five stories for *the New Yorker*. She is also credited with devoting years of her life to the comparative study of the Ancient Egyptian, Hindu, Wiccan, Gnostic, and Christian wisdom. She is introduced also as a pipe woman and a healer who studied under Paiute and Arapaho Medicine Men – as a bridge between the Indian wisdom of the heart and the Western wisdom of the mind. Eve arrived in what I will refer to as the Valley of Lost Borders in 1960. She states that she first began attending rituals and ceremonies in 1964, in the beginning as a sick white woman, and later as a friend, she hoped a trusted friend. Even though she had both Micmac and Maliseet blood, she never told me, and gave the impression to me that it was considerably less than my 1/16 Cherokee. For all I know she never mentioned it, so I think she was making an accurate description of how she was perceived in 1964, as a sick, white woman. She tells the story about her initial experiences and one old Paiute man who could not pass up the opportunity every time to walk near her and make deprecating comments about "white people". Some eight years later when a visitor from another tribe asked what that white woman was doing at the ceremony, her previous detractor responded by saying that "she's one of us, she's Paiute." She had been attending rituals and ceremonies for 13 years when I arrived.

Eve dealt with a variety of subjects in *the Snowy Earth Comes Gliding*, always drawing from her encyclopedic knowledge of symbolism. For the sake of simplicity and summation I will review six subject areas;

1) the Coso Range

2) the traditional Native American ecology and spiritual hierarchy

3) the Cry Dance

4) the Sun Dance, the Pipe, and the Sacred Hoop

5) the Ghost Dance

6) Miscellaneous ethnographic observations.

I do this because I was given the book and told to read it as part of my preparation before going to see the medicine man, and it is a summation of where Eve was, ten years after beginning her journey into Native American Shamanism.

THE COSO RANGE

Southeast of Lost Borders Valley and west of Death Valley, during the pluvial period at the end of the ice age there were four great lakes. The petroglyphs - rock carvings - there date as far back as 10,000 to

1,000 years ago. Must of these petroglyphs are at a minimum over two thousand years, and Coso Range has the largest concentration of any site in all of North America – estimated at 100,000, they have now identified and cataloged 35,000 petroglyphs. Since 1943 the Coso Range has been within the confines of the Naval Weapons Center. This is not thrilling to many traditionals (traditional Indians who respect the old ways) who would like to come and go at will, admission to the entire area of the petroglyphs being limited to guided tours provided by the Navy. At least the fences and Navy security have prevented that lamentably large and moronic segment of our population from scattering a place considered sacred since the time of Christ with beer cans and graffiti: 'Bob loves Sally' over irreplaceable and historic artwork.

Over the passage of time and with climactic and geologic change, the once abundant resources became scarce; the four great lakes became salt flats. In 1860 when the white man arrived, there were an estimated 100 Western Shoshoni and Paiute living there.

The word Coso is Shoshoni for the word fire, referring to the hot springs there, once reputed among the Indians for their healing power. The artwork takes various forms and depicts many subjects. Among the scenes depicted are men hunting with atlatls, bows, and dogs, men with Bighorn headdresses, ritual dancers, Medicine Men with medicine bags, and there are pictures of the Bighorn Sheep. There are other, more inexplicable pictures, and there are symbols, many of which are still used by Native Americans today. There is the circle, the circle bisected by the cross, the circle originating from a spiral, and the circle with eight spokes.

Eve states her opinion that as in the Lascaux Caves of France, the usual archeological explanation for such art is that it represents some form of "primitive" hunting magic, or possibly the more accurate, sympathetic magic. She states that explaining these works only in terms of hunting magic would be comparable to saying that the sign of the fish was used in the catacombs of Rome to promote a good catch among a simple fishing people. She acknowledges that some of the petroglyphs are probably for hunting magic, and others may have been to mark some historic occasion, but surely some of the symbols were used as mnemonic devices for the instruction and initiation of their shaman and the keepers of their wisdom.

The Bighorn Sheep is the predominant animal in all the petroglyphs on Coso Range. This equates in importance to the Buffalo for the Plains tribes. Both were the source of food, clothing, and ritual magic. For other tribes it was other animals, the Hare to the Algonquin, the Salmon and Reindeer to the Eskimos, the Beaver to the Micmac, other animals for other tribes, and was greatly revered Eagle by all tribes. She describes these as great supernatural beings, "Grandfathers," willing to give themselves body and blood to feed and sustain their people. She also notes that with the passage of time and the diminishing of the populations of these animals, either through natural climatic change like at Coso, through reduction of theses animal due to hunting for food, or through the encroachment of civilization and the dwindling of resources - the Grandfathers remain the same. At Coso Range, once the Bighorn were depleted and gone and in the plains when the Buffalo were wiped out, the Grandfather remain the same. In some of these places, due to government programs some of these wiped out animals are making a comeback. There are many more bison and wolves than there were decades ago, and there are efforts to bring back the Bighorn as well.

NATIVE AMERICAN ECOLOGY – A SPIRITUAL HEIRARCHY

The concept of the Grandfathers leads into the second subject area, what Eve terms the Indian ecology. The Indian ecology is inherently spiritual. The traditional Indians believe themselves to be relatives of the plants and animals they share the world with. They believe that everything created by the Great Spirit is equally important and has a rightful place. Her term for their outlook is that they understood the interdependence of all things. The traditional outlook is one of relating to plants and animals as people, whose welfare must be respected, for they have a voice in the affairs of the world, they have a voice heard by the Grandfathers.

For the sake of clarity I will jump ahead of my experiences of the time and try to present some conception of the spiritual hierarchy of the Native Americans. I do this for the main reason that others, as well as myself, who have studied and tried to understand these concepts for years often find themselves confused and unsure if their understanding has any validity. These concepts are not without analogy, in the East there are Hindu, Taoist, and Shinto analogies easily found, and in the West the Hebrew Kabbalah, and other traditions from Pre-Christian

Western Europe, represented by the Mystery Schools of ancient Greece and Rome, and the Druidic and Wiccan traditions are analogues. After Christianization, such analogies can be found in the writings of Paracelsus, and in more recent times the works of the poet W.B.Yeats, and Dion Fortune, and Israel Regardie.

The hierarchy presented is not of Native American origin, nor one taught by Eve, rather it is my tool for understanding developed primarily through experience, reading, and the process of analogy. There are seven levels of this hierarchy;

1) the Great Spirit,

2) the four creative forces - the Thunderbird,

3) the heavenly Grandfathers,

4) the archetypal Grandfather animal spirits,

5) the regional Grandfather animal spirits,

6) the individual animal spirits and the ghost of the dead,

7) The elemental spirits or beings of the elements such as water babies or giants.

The Great Spirit is the highest conception, the mother and father of all that is, within all things and containing all things within. This is the Great Holy, or the Great Mystery, and these names offer a description, the Great Spirit is not to be fully comprehended by humans, remaining a mystery, but describable as holy. The Great Spirit is sometimes referred to as Our Father or the Heavenly Father, and this usage was pronounced pre-Christian by the two Indians I heard use it.

The four creative forces are best explained by legends such as the one Eve used, that the Four Old Men were commanded by the Great Spirit to create the universe, and when they finished their work they were given charge of it. These Old Men dwell in the four corners of the universe in the East, South, West, and North. They are assigned four colors, but these vary among different tribes. The symbol used in the past as well as today is the circle quartered by the cross. The Plains tribes would use a sacred wheel or hoop in the Sun Dance, known as the Rehotti to the Northern Arapaho, it bore four inside makings known as the Hitanni, which symbolize the Four Old Men, the Keepers of the four world quarters, the four divides; summer, winter, day, and night, also the four elements; earth, air, fire, and water, and the four sets of eagle's tail feathers represent the Thunderbird.

So in sun Bear's system the cold northern winds being purification, the east wind of spring soothes and brings wisdom, the hot southern winds bring growth and healing, and the cool breezes of autumn brings on introspection to discover strengths and weaknesses.

Perhaps a clearer understanding will be brought through further analogy. In the Bible there are the four animals of Ezekiel. These are the bull, the man or angel, the lion, and the eagle. In Revelations 4:6 we find these beast "in the midst of the throne, and round and about the throne" of God. In other words, the seven lamps of fire burning before the throne "which are the seven spirits of God" of Revelations 4:5, are not as close to the Creator as the four beasts. In modern astrology as practiced in the West, these animals have an exact correlation. In the East is Aquarius, an air sign, in the south is Leo, a fire sign, in the west is the eagle of Scorpio, a water sign, and in the north is Taurus, an earth sign .In the Hebrew Kabbalah, there are four worlds; Atziluth, the boundless world of Divine Names, Briah, the Angelic world of Creations, Yetzirah, the Hierarchal world of Formations, and Assiah, the Elemental world of substances. (Hall, 1975)

These four powers or worlds were linked within the magic circle in the eyes of ritual practitioners prevalent at the turn of the last century in England, where people such as Israel Regardie and Aleister Crowley would work magical systems utilizing Judaic and Christian Symbolism and invoke these powers through the corresponding Archangel.

The Archangel of air in the east is Raphael, the Archangel of fire in the south is Michael, the Archangel of the west and water is Gabriel, and the Archangel of earth in the north is Auriel.

Eve goes on to say that the Morning Star is the messenger of the Four Creative Powers, the Four Old Men and that they are also referred to sometimes as the Thunderbird, who watches the world.

In myth the Thunderbird nests on a high mountain over un-scalable cliffs, his eyes capable of flashing lightning, his beating wings capable of thunder. The way she explains it the Thunderbird represents the creative forces, almost as a demiurge. I have heard the Thunderbird referred to as Thunderbird Eagle - Thunderbird Man. In this he is distinct from Grandfather Eagle, and appears equivalent to the logos, the creative word of God, not unlike the Hebrew Tetragrammaton, which is not only the Ineffable Name of God, but also considered the creative process. (Farrar, 1971)

Just as each plant and animal and human has a body and soul, so do the planets, the Moon, and the Sun, and the Stars. In the hierarchal level of heavenly Grandfathers will be the Mother Earth, our Father the Sun, Grandmother Moon, Grandfather Sky, the Morning Star, and the Star People. Each star is considered a person. Unlike the analogous European traditions, they do not personify these Grandfathers into gods and goddesses. When I asked a young Paiute about this, he saw no need for the concept. The Earth is our Mother as she is in her entirety. Rituals such as that of Wicca involving the invocation of a Goddess into the High Priestess, and her subsequent self-identification with the Moon Goddess are unknown. There are not gods and goddesses in their spiritual hierarchy. When a shaman works, he calls his personal spirit, known as a guardian spirit or an animal spirit. He may call his spirit, he may talk to his spirit, he may commune with his spirit, he may identify with his spirit, moving and sounding like the animal, and he may travel with his animal spirit, in a union of consciousness, but to my knowledge the shaman does not work personally with the heavenly Grandfather spirits, other than in prayer. Prayer is used but not invocation or self-identification. Prayer to the Morning Star, and the Mother Earth, to the Great Spirit and Heavenly Father are common among shaman today.

The Grandfather Animal Spirits can be thought of as the archetype and primal essence of the species they represent – and as the watcher and the of all members of that animal, as the watcher and guardian of those humans that have come into a relationship with that animal - and as the chief spirit of all such animal spirits. For example if the Great Spirit told the Four Old Men to make the world and they got to the American Great Plains and decided to make Buffalos, the Spirit in charge of Buffalos would be Grandfather Buffalo. He would be the first buffalo, and all buffalos would proceed from him. He would watch over the buffalos and the way humans treated them, and in what manner humans told myths about them. Grandfather Buffalo would look over and watch those families and clans, and individuals who developed special relationships with buffalos or buffalo spirits. Whether or not a buffalo spirit is the soul of a buffalo that has lived and died or whether there may be buffalo spirits that live in the spirit world and make associations through dreams and hearing those who fast or vision quest, I do not know. Whatever the true nature of a buffalo spirit, Grandfather Buffalo is the chief of all buffalo spirits. Grandfather Buffalo will send other buffalo spirits as his messengers and emissaries, as an Archangel would command an angel. Because all buffalo spirits represent and are under Grandfather Buffalo, a shaman may pray first to Grandfather Buffalo before addressing his own animal spirit. To add further confusion, a buffalo spirit might be the Grandfather of a region, and be called Grandfather Buffalo, when in actuality he is a sub-chief to the ultimate Grandfather Buffalo - his regional representative.

If the ultimate Grandfather Spirit is thought of as a general, and the individual, personal spirits are thought of as the ground troops, then the regional Grandfathers would be the middle range of authority, the captains and the colonels, and the majors. Eve points out that the regional Grandfathers are animals or even insects that play a predominant role in that region. A region noted for its beautiful flowers may be watched over by Grandfather Bee. In actuality it seems that the Indians today think that each region has more than one Grandfather watching over it. I was told repeatedly that before smoking the sacred Pipe, one should always invite the Grandfathers of that region to smoke with you, before lighting the pipe. It seems only logical that some animals, such as the Eagle, and the Buffalo, and the Bighorn Sheep would be prominent in those regions they populated, because of their magnificence. But in actuality, there is also Grandfather Mouse, Grandfather Hummingbird, and Grandfather Butterfly. The main difference in responsibility is that the regional

Grandfathers watch over all that lives in their region, not just those they have an established relationship with that animal. If the Spirit World is thought of as being much the same as the natural world, then many species may harmoniously intermix. A regional Grandfather may send aid to someone in a form not limited to one species. I have been in sweats where the medicine man would announce the presence of a spirit or spirits not summoned; twice I recall that spirits of different species came together like friends who had come to lend a hand. They were thanked at the end of the sweat, as were the regional Grandfathers who sent them, and the archetypal Grandfathers they represented.

The actual work of the shaman is done on the level of personal animal spirits. there are many terms used to describe this animal spirit, a shaman may say ; my spirit, my spirit power, my power, or refer to his spirit power by species, saying bear told me this, meaning his personal spirit, who is a bear spirit told him this. In my readings I have found many animals, and sometimes phenomena of nature may be a power. In the writings of anthropologist Julian Steward, and in the works of Eve can be found a plethora of such spirits.

Among these are Eagle, fox, bat, wolf, coyote, bear, buffalo, and Steward reports such things as mountains and the blue haze over the valley. Although Steward is reporting on the same tribe and area, it was some fifty years earlier. In my personal experience I can recall only one spirit who was a phenomenon of nature, and this spirit was capable of creating a bridge which would help the other animal spirits to come quickly. (Steward, 1974)

The shaman is the primary religious figure, and his fundamental work is that of healing. He performs this healing with the help of one or more spirits. Individuals other than the shaman may have a guardian spirit, but the shaman is distinguished by his greater experience and power. Illness can be of various causes. Good thoughts and deeds help nature, while bad thoughts and deeds, and dreams, or seeing a ghost can cause evil and sickness. Siskin lists sorcery, intrusion of disease objects, soul loss, and ghost as the most common. (Siskin, 1983) Steward relates the traditional Paiute belief in a soul, which would contain both the human soul and spirit, and a ghost, which does not go south with the soul, but remains in the land of the living, visiting people and serving witches. To heal his patient the shaman must diagnose the problem and take the correct actions. If the patient is sick from soul loss, the shaman will join in consciousness with his spirit power and go on a spirit journey to find and retrieve the lost soul. If illness is the result of sorcery, he may enter into a direct conflict, or preferably get the guilty party to remove the spell. If the sick have broken some taboo or offended an animal spirit by improper hunting or some other disrespect. the shaman will reveal this and offer some way to make amends. If the person is sick from a power intrusion the shaman with the aid of his spirit will suck it out of the patient thus healing them. If the person is sick from a dream the shaman will discover what the dream was, and he and his spirit will do what seems appropriate.

Paiutes receive their spirit powers through dreams, sometimes through inheritance, or through an intentional quest. Although the shaman of tradition is like the traditional Wiccan, able to bless or curse, able to heal or hurt, able to send his spirit to do his bidding as he sees fit, this idea has seemed to recede with the strong presence of Christianity on the reservations. Today it would seem the shaman is viewed primarily as a healer, no longer a specialist in harming as well as healing. I should note that the shaman doesn't coerce his spirit, but will request the spirit's aid humbly, as one would a friend. It is obvious that by analogy this level of personal spirits is the same as that occupied by the Angels and demons warring in the Judaic-Christian traditions. Like any war, the generals and colonels make the decisions and the troops fight the war.

Again to add to the confusion, the soul of a relative may come to and work with a shaman in the form of an animal spirit. The souls of the departed may be of help in other ways, without assuming the form of an animal spirit, and prayers to and for those who have passed on are said at every sweat.

The last level of this spiritual hierarchy is populated by the inhabitants of the elements; earth, air, fire, and water. Almost any reader will be familiar with tales of fairies and elves, of mermaids, and of giants. In the occult traditions of western Europe they were assigned names. The sylphs populated the air, the salamanders live in fire, the undines live in the water, and the gnomes populated the earth. These beings were referred to by occultist as the elementals, or as the elemental spirits. Although they may be visible and audible to humans, their existence is thought to be different than ours, because their bodies are made up of only the element they live in, while our bodies are composed of all four. The Paiutes have inhabited the earth with both giants and little people. The little people may take the traditional role of clown, doing everything backwards, and desiring to be addressed in this manner. If a little man from the mountains came to help at a healing sweat, the medicine man would say that he wasn't happy that the little man had come, hoped he wouldn't stay, hoped he had a terrible time. and surely hoped the little man would not do any healing. During the closing round the Medicine Man would say that he didn't thank him for what he'd done, and hoped he wouldn't come back. I know little about the giants, other than to ascribe them to the element earth. I have been places in the Valley of Lost Borders where there were huge rocks and sheer cliffs, and someone would say that giants lived there. I have never heard a giant called on as a spirit power, and know little else about them.

The Paiutes have populated the water with water babies. Siskin says that they live in the water, act, talk, and dress like people, except that they are two or two and a half feet tall, of either sex, with long hair, almost, but never touching the ground. They are pretty, having the same complexion as Indians and are said to have large broad hands. Generally, if anyone meets a water baby, they will lose consciousness immediately. They are said to travel clot, and that there little footprints are visible. Because they can travel on land but live in water, they can be found anywhere, and are said to like mountain lakes and streams. (Siskin, 1983) I have heard people mention water babies, but I have never heard them called on in sweats.

In the sweat, songs are song to the rocks and to the fire, so I have assumed that some form of spirit is thought to inhabit fire, and by extension, the air also. However, this is assumption, and I can offer no description of what the elementals of the air and fire might look like to the traditional Paiute.

Having concluded the description of this spiritual hierarchy, I should restate that this is not of native origin, and is primarily a tool for those unaccustomed to such ideas. Further, it is specific to the Paiutes and the Great Basin in general. There is often great variation among tribes, especially those separated by large distance, and those living in dissimilar environments.

The next subject area reviewed from *Snowy Earth Comes Gliding* is the Cry Dance. Eve explains how the prophet-dreamer Wovoka, early in his historical work condemned the burial practices previously practiced by the Paiutes. He insisted that the time had come for them to abandon their previous practices of killing horses, gashing skin with knives, of the women cutting off all their hair, of the burning of the diseased one's house and property. He stressed that they would all be reunited again anyway, so there was no reason for such over-whelming grief, and instituted the Cry Dance to substitute for the previous practices.

Before unnecessary confusion arises, some clarification may be needed in relation to Steward's claim that the traditional Paiutes believed in a ghost and soul. Remember in Eve's most simplified explanation the human is composed of a body maintained by a vital force, the chi, prana, mana, or whatever name. The emotional-mental aspect has an energy form called the aura, and the highest human spirit equates to the divine spark. By analogy in cultures and philosophies where this kind of division is found, the soul refers to the emotional-mental complex, and with it would go the divine spark. The energy matrix of the physical body; maintained or propelled by what could be thought of as unconscious memories, is the ghost that Steward claimed would visit the living and serve witches, and when seen, possibly cause illness.

For the sake of clarity, I will use the term wraith for the Body-ghost and the word ghost will mean a soul in contact with the living. The previous burial practices and those brought by Wovoka both aim to put the body to rest, and by cremation or coercion, put the physical ghost to rest, and send the soul, unhampered and undistracted on its way. While Steward said this was to the south, Eve says it was to set them free to travel the Milky Way, the road of the dead, to the Spirit World of the Grandfathers.

A Cry Dance is led by Cry Dance Singers, men who have forsaken drugs and alcohol, and who have not forgotten the traditional ways. They have either inherited their songs from a relative, received them while fasting and praying, or have been taught them by a (soul) ghost.

Eve describes the first Cry Dance she went to as she was just beginning to be accepted. Held next to the house of the deceased the night before his Christian burial the next day, the singers and mourners danced around a large fire, facing the fire was the deceased one's coffin, raised on a bier. The dancers danced all night, taking occasional breaks. The songs they sang changed, but the dance remained the same.

Because they were sending the soul away they danced counterclockwise, with their left side to the fire they would circle the fire and sing, dancing a step forward, half step back, balance, repeat. While they were dancing they all held strips of clothing that had belonged to the deceased.

Sometimes the cloth would be lifted high above their heads, but usually they were held in front. At some point during the night the widow was brought out of the house between two supporting men, and lead in front of the coffin.

In front of her loved one's coffin, in front of her family and community, she filled the silence of the night with her grief, described as a sad, lonely, noble, proud outburst of sorrow. As she cried into the night, the singers began to chant softly, while the family and mourners joined her lament. When it ceased there was a long silence and she was lead back into the house. After the widow went back inside the dancing and singing continued until first light at which time they turned inwards to the fire lifted high the pieces of cloth, and the hurled them into the fire. The ritual part concluded, everyone went inside to eat and drink coffee. This was preceded by a long grace in Paiute given by the head singer. At the conclusion of the meal, people went on their way, some to attend the Christian services later that day.

As Eve became more accepted she participated as a dancer at some Cry Dances, and described the emotional feeling of dancing as one that varied greatly, depending on the life and manner of death of the departed. The Cry Dance Singers used to receive new clothing as a gift and compensation for their work, Eve does not mention the modern form of compensation, a gap which I also am unable to fill.

The Sacred Pipe, the Sun Dance, and the Wheel are all part of the ritual complex of the Native American tribes of the Great Plains. Among these are the Lakota (Sioux) nations, the Cheyenne, and the Arapaho.

Although the origin myths about sacred objects such and the pipe and wheel; and about practices such as the Sun Dance vary among the tribes, their uses throughout the Great Plains form a unified ritual complex. The Pipe has been described, as has the wheel, which represents their people as a whole, and their relationship to the Great Holy.

The Sun Dance is a sacrificial ritual performed for the good of the people and of the planet. It involves the sacrifice of young men piercing their chest with leather thongs attached to the pole around which they danced until the thongs were pulled free, ripping their chest.

During the early 1900's the government burned the sacred regalia of these proud people and forbid the dance. The Sun Dance is again danced, the chest laceration, however is still forbidden by law.

The Arapaho and the Paiute live next door to each other and have enjoyed friendly relations for a long time, often attending the same boarding schools. They have also attended each other's rituals, and their Medicine Men are in contact with each other. The Paiute have the Sacred Pipe, but they do not have a Sacred Wheel representing their people in ritual and they do not practice the Sun Dance. This ritual complex is so thoroughly and beautifully described by Black Elk in Joseph Epes Brown's book, *The Sacred Pipe* as was the modern Arapaho Sun Dance by Eve, their restatement here would be superfluous. The Paiute are a people of the Great Basin, and the primary focus of their shaman was healing, past and present. They may have a great respect for the objects and rituals of other tribes, but the Sun Dance and the Wheel are not Paiute.

If the average American knows anything at all about the Paiutes it is probably in association with Wovoka and the Ghost Dance. In the terms of social science the Ghost Dance was a nativist movement, by Linton's typology, of the magical-revivalist variety. What the Ghost Dance was to the Anglos was absolutely terrifying - at least in concept. The Ghost Dance in simple terms was a prayer-dance that would bring paradise to the Indians, and leave the others non-existent.

Wovoka, also known as Jack Wilson, was born in Mason Valley, Nevada, sometime between the years of 1856-1858. He never left the area of his birth; those that sought his teachings came to him, which in part explains the diverse interpretations of his teachings.

He was a dreamer, a prophet, not a medicine man, at a time when all medicine men were required by the nature of their craft to have knowledge both benevolent and malevolent. Wovoka went into trance during an eclipse of the sun during January 1889, and remained in trance four days and nights. When he revived he said he had seen the Great Holy and all those who had died in another world, and that Numin'a told him to teach the dance and that if it was danced properly the dancers would be able to go to that other world as he had, and see their loved ones. He taught them the Spirit Dance of the Other World.

Perhaps the fact that the U.S Army had dispatched so many of those dead was a factor in the way they reacted (see the Wounded Knee Ghost Dance Massacre.) As time passed and the teaching spread and disseminated among various nations the Ghost Dance changed and evolved. Instead of the dance allowing the dancers to visit the dead in the other world as it was originally meant to do, a belief rose that dancing the dance would bring back the dead. Eve relates James Mooney's version of the Ghost Dance doctrine, as he supposedly heard it in 1892. The whole red race, living and dead would be united on a regenerated earth, living in paradise with no death, disease, or misery. The white race would have no part in this, and would disappear with the other worn out and unnecessary things of the world.

Wovoka taught them to do the dance at least every six weeks, to do no harm, to do right always, to work with and get along with the whites and the Great Spirit would take care of everything.

But, he taught emphatically, there must be no fighting, they must not make war. As stated previously spoke out against the brutality and waste of their burial practices, and introduced the Cry Dance.

The Ghost Dance was danced for four nights and the mourning of the fifth day. It was danced clockwise, alternately sexed, holding hands, facing the fire and singing. It was the same step of the Cry Dance, sometimes called the dragging dance. The dancers would paint their faces with an ochre color. The Paiutes would sing their slow, lilting, powerful songs, while wearing emblems of the Thunderbird, and feathers of the Magpie.

Because many tribes sent representatives and medicine men, at different times, there are many variations on the Ghost Dance doctrine. The derivations can be categorized by four criteria:

- tribe,

- emphasis,

- method of change,

- Fate of the whites.

The Paiutes emphasized the Thunderbird, the eagle, the crow, and the Sage hen. The change would either be brought about by flood, while the Indians waited in the mountains for four days. Their alternate was that a re-born earth - new and white as though covered with snow - would come gliding over the old earth, driven by a whirlwind.

The game and all the dead would be reborn, the whites and all the old things would vanish. The unfaithful Indians would either be turned into dwarfs a foot tall, or turned into wood, or stone.

The Shoshoni thought everyone would go e faithful would awaken in four days to a world reborn. The Arapaho, the Kiowa, and the Cheyenne all thought it was the end of an Age; and the beginning of a new Age. They thought the earth, the grass, the trees, and the people were all too old and worn out. The Arapaho stressed the Crow and the Thunderbird, and thought when the change came they would be lifted to safety by their sacred dance feathers.

The change would either come as earth sliding from west to east, as one hand would slide over another, or else be brought by a wall of fire. If it came by gliding earth, they and the whites would be resurrected in separate worlds, if it came by fire, the fire would drive the whites back to their original homeland, and then be put out by twelve days of rain. The Cheyenne stressed the crow and thought the change would come by sliding earth, and that they would be raised by their sacred dance feathers, and remain unconscious for four days. Then they would awaken on a world reborn, and find that they and the whites had become one people. The Kiowa stressed the coming spirit army, believed in the gliding earth and being lifted by the feathers, but expected the resurrection of Indians only. The Sioux expected the total annihilation of the whites, and stressed the eagle, crow, buffalo, and the Ghost Dance Shirt.

The Sioux historically are a people much more given to warfare than the Paiutes. They had suffered greatly at the hands of the White man, as it could be argued that the traditionals were still suffering. The Lakota chose to ignore Wovoka's strong injunction against warfare. The Lakota wore a garment known as the Ghost Dance Shirt. This concept is not Paiute, nor does it come from Wovoka. Eve hypothesizes that with the strong presence of the Mormons, the idea of the Mormon Endowment robe which shields the wearer against evil, was put together with the coming immortality of the Indians, and the power of the Ghost Dance, and the result was the Ghost Dance Shirt.

The Sioux, with an almost Middle Eastern kind of logic, ignored Wovoka`s injunctions and reasoned if the Great Spirit was going to remove the whites from the face of the earth anyway, why not hasten the day with a holy war. Furthermore, why should He have all the fun anyway, they had suffered, it was only fair that they should take part in the retribution. The Sioux believed that if a shirt was properly consecrated and worn through the four nights and the morning of dancing, the wearer would be invincible, and the Ghost Dance Shirt would be bullet proof.

The settlers and the army were not ignorant of the Ghost Dance. The very idea that someone is performing witchcraft, or sorcery, or attempting to pray a victim(s) to death quite often brings on an irrational reaction in the intended victim. In Hawaii where the Kahunas were reputed to practice a death prayer, the very rumor that such work was being performed might cause the intended victim to attempt a preemptive strike, or to lie down and die. The white settlers may not have belied in the power of the native medicine men, but they were certainly aware that the natives did. This awareness, plus their own biblical traditions of the Israelites being saved from treatment not dissimilar to their treatment of the Indians, plus rumors that the dreaded Sioux nations were about to go back on the warpath, drove the setters to state of high anxiety. Fear plus irrational fear can bring about the worst kind of human behavior, which is a mild description of the horror and massacre known in history as the battle of Wounded Knee.

Wovoka was disgusted at the violent perversion of his teachings and the ensuing tragedies, for Wounded Knee was not the only reaction or act of retaliation. Eve simply states that it brought on bitter tines for the Paiutes because they were the source of the Ghost Dance. The Paiutes today remember those bitter times. She does not document this statement, and says that Paiutes she knew would not even acknowledge that there had even been a Ghost Dance or a prophet Named Wovoka. Having grown up in the South, hearing the Civil War stories passed down from one great-grandfather, and hearing the remembrances of another too young to fight, who told his children and his children`s children about watching the long walk home of the defeated, shoeless, wounded, limping hungry remnants of once proud fighting men; I have little doubt that that Paiute tales of bitter times have been passed down the generations.

After Wounded Knee the Ghost Dance was outlawed. Some claimed that because the Sioux had broken faith with the true Ghost Dance teachings, that the deliverance was either cancelled, or postponed indefinitely. Some just quit believing, while others may have quietly continued.

Although Eve repeatedly says that no living Paiute would talk to her about the Ghost Dance, and her record of the songs from an ethnographic report to the Smithsonian circa 1892-3, and her other information is from accounts of the time, she goes on to state that she believed the Ghost Dance was still being practiced. This statement alone, as well as some others, made her and her book unpopular among certain people; some of whom had previously had been much more friendly. Because the Ghost Dance was still illegal in 1977, and if the people were still so sensitive that they wouldn`t talk about it, and if they remembered and retold stories of past persecutions, then it is not surprising that some people didn't like her book. She gave real locations, she used a few real names, she used some photographs she had taken; and she had stated her opinion that there were Paiutes still doing the Ghost Dance. There were those that thought she had made some severe mistakes.

So they told her, in the future, no real names, no photographs, no real locations, no Ghost Dance nonsense, and this goes for all the people you bring, too. Those were the conditions I accepted before I could go to the sweat lodge.

Her book was not the only reason things were kept quiet. Technically, the sweat lodge rituals we were participating in were against the law. This was surprising to me, and I imagine it would be to that mythical normal American. Since so many of the Europeans who came to this continent and displaced the native, population, came fleeing religious persecution, and went on to guarantee themselves religious freedom in their constitution I was angrily amazed to find that the Native Americans had been denied the right to practice their own religion as they saw fit. I have been in heated arguments with patriotic Americans who could scarcely believe, even when shown, that Congress did not grant the Native American population the right to practice their religion, legally, until 1978. Even with that change, the traditional Sun Dance is still illegal.

There were many people who attended sweats who were also devout Christians, finding no conflict between them. But that certainly did not mean that the church communities on the reservations approved of or condoned such activity. The easiest way to avoid problems and social pressure was just to keep things quiet. There seemed to be a pervasive feeling that if someone was in need of the sweat, that they would find their way there. One hundred years of persecution are not forgotten in five or ten years, and the South is not the sole home of the cross burning mentality.

The final subject area to be reviewed from Eve's book is her ethnographic observations, although she would not have referred to them as such. This miscellaneous collection is divided between comments about the Paiutes, their feelings and attitudes, and comments on their sacred mysteries and the phenomenon associated with their practice.

Eve relates such practices as "going behind the blanket" and the "go slow Way". Going behind the blanket is when person enters into a personal silence and becomes oblivious to the outer and bothersome world. The go slow way could also be called the no show way, it is the attitude of waiting, not being hasty to react, not giving your own thoughts or emotions away. She lists the virtues that seem most admired. The embodiment of which would be a person who is: honest, just, generous, frank and concise. The Indians have never understood the seeming neurotic need of the white man to constantly hear the sound of his own voice. Their saying that "no flies come into a closed mouth" epitomizes this attitude. Besides the incessant chatter of whites, there is a deep resentment against writers, photographers, archeologists, and curious probers of whatever variety. She retells what an old Paiute told her one time about the possibility of taping some sacred songs.

He told her, "A song is made to be born, and heard by those who are meant to hear, and then it dies on the air." (Eaton,1974,p.56) Their attitude seems to be that Life is sacred and meant to be lived, not caught still on photographs or tapes. Still, those questioning, seeking, and searching who come in humility, with a sincere desire to learn, and a respect for the Indian traditions and ways may find what they seek. The examples range from the two men who recorded and brought to the world Black Elk`s knowledge and vision to Eve. Although she took a lot of flak for her first book; she continued on in that community and wrote two additional books on her journey into shamanism.

The Indians have an ethic against waste. Hunting is done in a sacred manner, with prayers for the animal before and after a swift and merciful kill. There is the idea that if you don't use what the Grandfathers give you, it will be taken away. Also, anything that can be used rightly can also be used wrongly, such as power objects like the sacred pipe. Paiutes are known historically to raise and keep only three animals, the dog, the horse, and in the past the Medicine men would keep two or four eagles like pets, for the purpose of supplying sacred eagle feathers. Today Paiutes are still noted for their horsemanship, yet cows are rare on reservations. Cow's milk is not a prized Paiute food, and beef is considered not as good as venison and drastically inferior to buffalo. The result is many Paiutes making a living tending cows, but they won't raise them for their own use.

Indians have never understood the white man's need to conquer the new world. They had always lived here at home in their home, this wilderness in need of conquest .Obviously they saw themselves as proud and noble people defending their sacred land against the savages who invaded it. They have also never understood the American outrage at notorious historical figures like Adolf Hitler; did he treat the Jews and Gypsies so differently than the U.S. government treated them? There is an attitude that the conquest of the Mother Earth with bulldozers and strip mines, and all the nasty ugly pollution is a desecration against the Earth, and it will be paid for.

In 1971 when there were earthquakes near Los Angeles, a Paiute warned Eve that if no birds were seen in the skies for three days she should go to the mountains. Maybe they really were still dancing, or maybe they thought payment had come due in some other form.

The Indians have their own concept of time, which is not an hourly way of thinking about time, it is doing things when the time is right. Other observations Eve made were that the Arapaho and Cheyenne have only one color term for the colors we call blue and green.

Also Paiutes call the little whirlwinds of the desert "dust devils," a term they take seriously, telling you not to look at them for that will attract them to you.

Eve relates how reticent the Paiutes are to talk about their sacred mysteries, except at the ceremonies themselves. They have a strong feeling that such things should only be discussed when the time was right. Part of this, other than a cultural inclination may be the belief that by talking about spirits and powers, you attract their attention, or invoke them, which should only be done with purpose and intention. She describes phenomenon associated with participation in the rituals, these were primarily her sensations of the talons of a large bird on her arms and shoulders, hearing the beating wings of a flying bird inside where no bird could be, also hearing the whistle of an eagle, not the sound of the eagle whistle used in ritual, but the authentic sound of a real bird, where no bird should or could have been. She says such phenomenon has been explained away as mass hypnosis, but she disagrees. She notes the strange phenomenon of knowing how to sing the Paiute songs while in the sweat lodge, but not being able to recall them later. She comments on a seeming surplus of intuition, having questions answered before she could ask them. She also comments on birds as the bringers of messages and as omens - that when a bird or birds appear one should greet them verbally or mentally and use one's intuition and knowledge of the bird's qualities to figure out what the message is.

As mentioned Eve gave me *Snowy Earth Comes Gliding* to read before I went to go see the Medicine Man. After reading it again to prepare this review I see that I didn't read it that carefully, or else I didn't understand it thoroughly, or just did not have the experiences yet to put it in context. I remember understanding by analogy about the four powers, and I understood that a Grandfather and the animal spirits were analogous to the Archangels and angels. Most of what I called her ethnographic comments was immediately forgotten, because it seems I relearned most of them through my own experience.

My defense for a less than studious initial reading of *Snowy Earth* is based on the strong feeling I experienced at the time that I had spent years reading and I was eager to get right to the doing instead of more reading. Within the span of my first week my daily routine of study, conversation, and prayer was established and my preliminary meeting with the medicine man was arranged. Every day Eve and I would smoke the sacred pipe and have long discussions, often taking a question and answer format. This would usually take place on the nearby mountain, or sitting in Iren's flower garden. Every second or third day Eve would perform her healing practices as I sat passively in my wheelchair. To the other new disciplines was added the instruction that I keep a daily journal, which was to be a record of my dreams and significant life experiences, especially those of a spiritual nature.

As I wrestled with analogy in my quest for understanding, I recall a certain amount of confusion regarding the nature of what a spirit or spirit power really was. Before Eve came into my life, my exposure to the term spirit was in connection with very dubious séances and spirit mediums. My initial attempt at understanding had me combining images of Casper the friendly ghost with images of the giant insects of Carlos Castaneda. When Eve told me that there was a powerful spirit associated with her sacred pipe, I began to understand when I witnessed the regular appearance of large birds of prey when she smoked. She told me how she could sometimes feel the talons of her spirit animal as it sat on her shoulder. From this I at least concluded that an animal spirit was conceived of, and perceived as having the form of an animal and existing in some relationship with physical, living members of that species. Eve told me to accept the real birds as emissaries sent by her spirit eagle, which as was previously mentioned, she believed to be a red tailed hawk.

I would sometimes experience profound states of well-being while involved in smoking the sacred pipe or being worked on during healing. These states were neither visionary nor hallucinatory, and were not accompanied by strong physical sensations, other than an occasional light headedness, while smoking, which may have been attributed to the mental state of prayer, or nicotine intoxication. Eve and Edie both told me that healing would begin on a spiritual level, and then on a physical, and that the beginning work was not expected to be other than spiritual.

From conversations with Eve in Georgia and conversations with Edie in California I was aware that Eve considered the sweat lodge ritual to be a powerful form of healing. I didn't ask that many direct questions about Eve's health to Eve, it seemed impolite. I did gather from my reading and conversations with Edie that Eve had health problems in 1964-5 when she began attending ceremonies. She had a minor problem with a recurrent growth on her eyelid. Doctors would remove it and it would grow back .A medicine man removed it with a gourd during a ceremony, one of the first proofs of the healing potential of the American shaman in her personal experience.

The eyelid, although was a very minor problem, Eve had cancer. She had heard her death sentence pronounced repeatedly by doctors who did not doubt the accuracy of their test, or their inability to keep her alive much longer. As said, she was to hear this repeatedly, and she repeatedly refused to listen.

While preparing this paper in the spring of 1985 I ran into my lawyer, Joe Harmon. He had gone to visit Eve also, not simultaneously with my visits, but in the same time frame. Of course our conversations turned to Eve, and he related to me one of the many stories about Eve's defeat of the monster we call cancer.

"The stogy I remember," Joe said," was that the stuff would come, she would go through the ceremonies, and it would go away. When I was out there, she had recently overcome another recurrence of cancer. I heard she had gone to a doctor who was an old friend of hers and a contemporary in age. His diagnosis was stomach cancer, and his judgment was that an operation was immediately necessary.

So they went in surgically and laid open her stomach. In the doctor's opinion, there was nothing he could do, the cancer was prevalent throughout her stomach, if he cut it all out, there would be no stomach left. He sewed her back up, after he concluded she did not have long to live.

"When she had recovered from the surgery and her doctor friend came to tell her the results, the man broke down and cried. He told her how advanced the cancer was, how he could do nothing, and how she should get her affairs in order, she had on the outside chance, three months left. She put her arm around the doctor, and comforted him, and she told him everything was going to be alight."

Joe and I sat there, and smiled, neither of us had dry eyes, and in silent communion, we shared our respect and love for this woman who was a fighter, for her own health, and that of others. As I looked around, I became aware of the others in the room who had been quickly listening to our conversation. Without their asking, I knew they wanted to know the outcome of the story, so I told them. "Eve went to the Medicine Men, she went through the ceremonies, and she went on a very strict diet. She beat, cancer that time, as she had since 1965, and she beat it again, later, every time it raised its ugly head. When Eve finally did pass on, some six years after her three month death sentence, she was over eighty, and she died of heart failure."

So in 1977, when Eve told me that the sweat lodge was a powerful way of achieving healing and transformation, she was talking from her heart, from the conviction of her own experience. Besides the other things mentioned; upon my arrival Eve began to set in motion the events that would terminate in my first four day healing sweat.

Eve informed me that I would have to go meet the man who ran the sweat lodge, whom I will refer to as E.R. Strong. I had to go talk with him as a preliminary, and if things went well, I would ask him for a four day healing sweat. Eve told me that if things went well enough for me to ask for the sweats, there was still no guarantee as to how he would react. He might say yes or no, outright, or he might wait to decide, he might say yes but not set the time; or he could say yes and set an immediate date. She warned he might invite me to the weekly Sunday sweat and check me out before deciding about the four day healing sweat. She warned me that there were just no guarantees; that it was out of her hands, but she bolstered my confidence telling me that E.R. had taken the same oath she had, to heal the sick. By tradition a medicine man can decide as he sees fit, but Eve felt the oath was open, without limitation, that the work of a healer was to heal those who came asking.

She told me when I talked to him to speak clearly, and that whatever I asked him for, do so only once. I knew as she prepared me for the visit some 57 miles north of Freedom, that she had likewise prepared E.R. and his wife for my coming. I have no doubt that Eve relied on her thirteen year relationships, and brought to their attention Ruth`s reports on my initial workings as a healer, and the fact that I had traversed the width of the continent, hoping. Edie assured me not to worry, that Eve had really gone to bat for me and it would all work out.

I was a mass of anxiety and excitement on that 57 mile ride north to for my first meeting with E.R. Strong. Eve and Edie answered my last minute questions as we drove up on a bright autumn afternoon. Magnificent scenery and interesting conversation made the ride seem quick, I had never seen a desert valley so beautiful. The Valley of Lost Borders is about 180 miles long and about 30 miles wide, running north-south. On its western side rise of the Sierra Nevada Mountains, where stand some of the highest mountains in the continental United States. On the east side of the valley rises the To`sava Nagiti mountains, in the center of the valley runs the Pata River down into Lake Pa`tsiyata. The highway, coming up from L.A. headed parts northward, runs parallel but not adjacent to the river. The highway runs up past Lake Pa`tsiyata, which long ago was once a large lake, but is now more salt flats surrounding a small lake. The highway runs directly through the four population centers, which I refer to as towns, but that may be misleading. These towns are really a few stores and shops on either side of the highway, and the small roads and houses around them. Although

Cardinal has a population above five thousand, the other three towns range from the mid-hundreds to around fifteen hundred. All of these have a minimum of two or three gas station-convenience stores, a restaurant, a bar, a general store, and a church. Freedom and Big Tree are the smallest, Freedom was once a fort and now is the county seat. Big Tree seemed to be the population center with the largest Native population. Wako`po is the southernmost town, ten miles north of the lake. It is slightly larger than Freedom, which lies thirty miles north. Freedom has the courthouse, a school, and a storefront bank open twice a week. Big Pine is fifty-seven miles north of Freedom; and Cardinal is thirty miles north of Big Tree. Cardinal is the only town with any depth off the main road, and looks like any small American towns, complete with banks that open seven days a week and all the fast food chain restaurants.

Besides a small lumber and building supply warehouse in Wako`pi and a few mountain fisheries, there were no signs of industry. Eve and

Edie explained to me some of the realities of this area's demographics.

They surprised me with a certain amount of bitterness as they explained the folklore and history of what they and the local population called "the jobless valley." The reason for their bitterness they explained; was the loss of youth they saw and felt as inevitable. This was as true for the local Indian and whites, as well as the young people who moved into the area and later moved away. The two reasons for this one-way flow of people is the lack of available employment or private land. It makes since that young people will not stay where there is no place to work or live.

They told me what I call a folk lore-historical explanation. The Paiute and White cultures did not collide until the 1860's and they did not get off on the right foot. From later readings I found that the white intruders thought of them as the most primitive of all Indian s, probably because they ate insects. The Paiutes had a low opinion of whites, having observed the behavior of the first few wagon trains that ventured into the area. They kept their distance and watched these strange new people as they struggled across. Caught by the snow without adequate food supplies, and lacking the necessary survival skills, many died and those surviving were in danger of starving to death, so they ate their dead. The Paiutes found this unnecessary, revolting, and bizarre behavior.

When the whites came in force they took the well watered land to raise their cattle and they took the mountains with minerals. The "active hostilities" lasted only a few years, the Paiutes being a nation of very small population, widely dispersed in small bands, and possessing few horses. So the settlers got the choice lands, the government took the rest, and the Paiutes got corralled on the reservation.

Although their land was stolen and they were put on the reservation, the Paiutes, except for the Ghost Dance era, were not as badly treated, abused, and debased as some of the other tribes. Part of this may have been because the Paiute quickly earned a reputation as exceptionally skilled horsemen who made excellent ranch hands. In the Valley of Lost Borders from the times when the ranches and farms were begun, up until the 1930's, there an abundance of successful ranches and farms.

They asked me had I seen the movie *China Town* and considering their ages and all the movies they had seen before my time, I made sure it was the one starring Faye Dunaway and Jack Nicholson before I answered in the affirmative. Among other plot lines in the movie, one of the plots is the move by a power hungry, farsighted, greedy and ruthless business man played by John Houston, who directs the acquiring of water rights by a Los Angeles utility company which he owns large shares of and controls. Eve and Edie told me that the movie was based on fact, that in their valley there were unexplained deaths and burnings, and that in real life the utility company had given farmers and ranchers an offer they couldn't refuse. There was a memorable scene in the movie where there is a long chase in an orchard, when hostile farmers mistake Nicholson for a utility company henchman. According to local people that farm was supposed to be in the southern part of their valley. Whatever the truth, pressure was put on local farmers and ranchers to sell either their land outright, or sell the water rights to their land. However it came about, there is little privately owned land in the valley, most is owned either by state or federal government by a utility company supplying water to LA. I have seen long abandoned orchards in the southern part of the valley, the dry and withered fruit trees still in line, and it is a fact that most of the valleys` water goes south. In fact, on the fifty seven mile drive north to Big Tree, there is only one area of productive farmland, and it has a creek running through it.

They explained that since L.A. got the water that would supply the ranches and farms, and that other than jobs with the utility company overseeing land and canals, and wildlife and fishery jobs with the state, which were limited in number, then just weren`t any jobs in the valley. They didn`t foresee much change in the job situation in the future.

As we drove up I looked around thinking about water, and its` incredible importance in cycles of life. In the valley there is an obvious difference in the amount of precipitation that falls on the two mountain ranges. The reason for this is that the 14,000 ft. Sierras catch most of the water coming from the Pacific Ocean. The moisture in the air to a great extent is trapped by these snow covered mountains, leaving the land east of them much more arid than that lying between the Sierras and the Pacific. The western side of the Sierras shows the evidence of much greater rainfall than the eastern side adjacent to the valley. The Sierras are magnificent, snowcapped, dotted with pine trees, jutting with huge sharp rock formations. The Ta`sava Nagiti across the valley has few trees, is not high enough to be snowcapped, and has a reddish brown appearance. The valley floor is sandy, with few trees other than around the streams and river, and the long standing population centers.

I mentioned to Eve and Edie the vast difference of emotional feeling one could experience while viewing the beauty of Nature. Being familiar with the Appalachian Mountains which are covered with oak, and maple, and pine and overflowing with wildlife, these mountains seemed so desolate. Whereas the mountains of the south had always represented in my mind, and invoked from my emotions deep appreciation for the nurturing aspect of the Earth Mother, these mountains seemed more masculine, an environment not so much nurturing as challenging, bespeaking eloquently the struggle for life.

This is not to say that the mountains and the desert valley between them are lifeless. As was immediately pointed out to me, and as I had already noticed, the area was far from lifeless. The valley has numerous streams coming down from the mountains and the sandy floor is filled mostly with sage plants and other bushes, ranging from knee level to above human height. Besides the smaller animals like lizards and rodents and such which I assumed to be there, I had noticed in my head lights at night a healthy rabbit and white-tail deer population. During the days I had noticed, besides a variety of smaller birds, many hawks, crows, buzzards, and I was watchful for the Golden Eagles said to populate the area.

Before we got to Big Tree we pulled off the highway and turned onto the Paiute land. We went down dirt roads past a couple of small Christian churches that were of the holiness and fundamentalist varieties. We pulled into our destination after a few turns and my anxiety hit new highs. As we got out I could see the igloo shaped sweat lodge, standing behind a wall of stacked stone, roofing sheet metal and plywood. There were several outbuildings, and various pieces of farm equipment scattered around the yard, and we made our way to a small wood house, nestled under three trees which shaded a cool and grassy front yard.

I was introduced to E.R. and his wife Maria and we went inside. E.R was a large man, well above six feet, with powerful arms and thick through his chest and shoulders. He had dark hair, was a strikingly handsome man, and looked a decade younger than his sixty-four years. His wife Maria was of a more normal size, but was reputed to possess an uncommonly sweet disposition. I had been told that she was a devout Christian, and although she did not participate in the rituals inside the sweat lodge, she helped with the support work outside if needed and always helped with and attended the ceremonial meal which always follows a sweat.

Eve wanted E.R. to show me some of the figures he had sculptured from pipestone. These carves figures were of a symbolic nature, mostly of animals and of men praying. Some were simply done, emphasizing their symbolic nature, while others were intricately carved. Eve told me that some of his work was on display at an Indian university and also at a regional museum. After appreciating this artwork, E.R. and I went outside for a talk.

E.R. does not speak the grammatically perfect English of a college graduate, but he speaks it well and uses it as his primary language. He walked beside me and I rolled my wheelchair over towards the sweat lodge. He led me in conversation by saying a few words and then letting me roll with it. He said something to the effect of "so you come all the way from Georgia..."

So I filled in that I had come from Georgia to visit Eve, to learn and be healed. He asked me about the nature of my injury and the extent of my function and abilities. I remember being unsure if he had understood me correctly when I was explaining that although my legs were paralyzed the injury and disruption of function was located in the nerves of my spinal column. Nevertheless, we both knew why I was there and he didn't seem to be avoiding the subject of health and healing, so I went for it. I told him I had come from Georgia hoping that he would allow me into the sweat lodge and that I could go through the four day healing sweat.

I sat there and he stood there for what seemed like a long time. He was looking out towards the fields but he seemed lost in thought. Eve had told me in no uncertain terms; that once I asked to keep my big mouth shut. She told me after I asked not to repeat it, not to mention it, just ask, and wait. Finally he turned to me and said" O.K., You have four day sweat, starting Friday night, ending Monday night. Eve`ll tell you what you need to bring. Just pray, cry out, Grandfathers hear you, take pity, but pray hard, cry out from the heart. You`ll be o.k."

We drove home during a beautiful sunset, elated that things had gone so well. Eve told me she had thought I would get the sweats, but she was surprised he had agreed so quickly and set such an immediate date.

They explained that since the sweats were for **me** that I would have to provide the food and the ritual gifts. My family was responsible for the fire wood and for the cooking on all four days. They told me that it was a load not to be taken lightly, but not to worry, that they would stand behind me as my family.

On our way home that evening I mentioned that E.R. had seemed to light up a little when I told him that at least one of my direct ancestors was a full blooded Cherokee, my grandfathers' grandmother. I was later to find out my grandmother was part Creek Indian as well. Eve told me what I was to hear again, that some Indians think a little blood goes a long way. She said that her blood certainly hadn't impeded her progress, and added an aside to the effect that E.R. was not pure Paiute but thought to have some French-Mexican-Paiute on one side of his family.

I had talked with Eve and Edie and some of the local townspeople trying to get a handle on the racial relationships of the area. I was to hear some comments that reminded me the situation was not dissimilar to that of the South. Among the various comments and answers were things such as, "white women don`t ever go on the reservation alone," "white kids don`t go the reservation after dark," when I asked if there were fights, ` sometimes the high school kids have fist fights along racial lines," when I asked if there was much Anglo-Indian dating in the integrated high schools, "it happens sometimes, not too often, it`s frowned on."

I knew from observation as well as conversation that like the blacks of the South or the Chicanos of the Southwest, that the Paiutes represented the lower side of the economic scale in the valley, on the average their houses were not as big, their cars and trucks not as new, and they were not dominate in local politics or law enforcement. The situation seemed to be much like at home. Integration may be a legal reality, but you can't regulate hate, some people are bigots, some aren't. Legal equality and integration may be legal facts; but economic equality and equality of opportunity are not brought about just by laws but by work and time. There is much work and time to go before the Valley of lost Borders becomes a totally integrated, economically balanced social paradise. But on the surface the relations between the Anglos and Paiutes did not seem that bad, did not seem hostile to a stranger.

I was aware that an integrated sweat lodge was much more the exception than the rule, on any reservation, anywhere. Eve had told me that E.R.'s sweat was considered something of an experiment by the other medicine men in the region. The process had begun in 1965 when Eve began attending ceremonies in search of healing, and she had received that healing and become more accepted with the passage of time. When R. Harris, now dead, who at the time was a friend and teacher of E.R., and one of the healers Eve had gone to, asked Eve what she wanted, she responded that she wanted to be a healer of miseries great and small. Harris decided that she should have a Sacred Pipe and go through the' sweats and fasts that would make her a Pipe Healer. Harris directed E.R. to carve her pipe, and when it was finished, Harris presented it to her and instructed her in its use.

E.R. had not always been a shaman but had begun as a pipe carver and from there graduated into becoming a Pipe Healer and running a sweat lodge. Harris had officiated over their fasts, but E.R. had begun the process before Eve. The process consisted of three fasts, which were preceded by and concluded with a sweat lodge.

The fast is from all food and water, and the faster remains alone, without human communication. They may nap during the day but must remain awake throughout the night, praying. The first fast is for two nights and one day, the second is for three nights and two days, the third is for four nights and three days.

Eve had finished her fasts before Harris passed away, but because of the distance at which he lived, Eve had been guided in her development by E.R., among others. E.R. had guided Eve in her understanding of and in her relationship with her animal spirit.

Eve had acquired the implements of her craft and learned how to use them, and had been called upon by E.R. to work on him one time when he was sick. Because she had proved herself by meeting the challenges of becoming a Pipe Healer, she was allowed to bring her friends who were sick and then those she thought suitable to meet E.R,, and if he approved, to sweat. So one by one E.R.`s sweat lodge had become integrated, at least what could be called selectively integrated.

When Eve was asked by Grandfather Harris what she wanted she responded that she wanted to be a healer of misereres great and small. So Grandfather R. Harris, who had trained E.R Strong and decided that she should have a pipe and go through the sweat lodges and fasts to make her a Pipe

Healer.

E.R. carved the Pipe as directed by Harris and Eve acquired the implements of her craft and developed a relationship with her animal spirit. Because Harris lived at some distance towards the east and E.R. lived in Lost Borders Valley, much of her development, especially her understanding and relationship with her animal spirit was guided by E.R. Strong.

Because Eve bravely met the challenges of becoming a Pipe Healer and proved herself to the medicine men she was allowed to bring sick whites and people she thought needed healing to meet E.R. and if he approved, to the sweats. By the time I arrived in 1977, some twelve years after she had begun regular attendance, there were at least nine other whites, or Anglos, a term I heard used often, who were accepted in the sweats. These were Edie, April and Bill, Gunter and Ingrid, Donna and Gabe, Eva and Marilyn. Of these, Bill worked with E.R. doing maintenance for the local school system, and Gunter was learning to be a singer. I often heard Bill referred to as E.R.'s adopted son. Although there were probably other Anglos who had come or would come when in the area, these nine were the ones who lived in the area and attended regularly. By regular attendance I don't mean that all nine were there at every sweat, but at any sweat you could expect to find between three to six of these people. April and Bill, Donna and Gabe, and Marilyn were all in their mid-twenties or early thirties. Eva may have been slightly older, and Gunter and Ingrid were middle age, with adolescent and college age children.

I had already met most of the Anglos who attended sweats and was thankful when several stepped forward to help me fulfill my responsibilities for having requested the four day healing fast.

These responsibilities were of two categories. The first was that of getting the presents and other required objects, the second was acquiring the food and being responsible for organizing who would do what.

This seemed like a lot of activity at the time, but I'm probably making it out to be more hectic than it was. The problem was not getting the food or gifts but organizing who would do what in such a short space of time. A sweat lodge is small and round and comfortably can feel full with anywhere from eight to twelve people, with an absolute maximum of about eighteen. Eve told me that since that sweats had been announced so quickly, and I was unknown in the valley, a safe bet would be to prepare food for about ten to twelve, with the exception of Sunday when more could be expected because it was a previously announced regular Sunday sweat.

I followed Eve's suggestions on everything concerning the preparations. She told me there were three people serving functions in the sweat who must be given presents. The first of these is the medicine man, and Eve said I must get him four separate presents. She told me he smoked and suggested I get him a couple of cartons of

Winstons, and two cans of tobacco. I was to give these presents all before the first sweat, and if I was so inclined, I would put an envelope on the mound in front of the eastern door, with whatever I felt comfortable with as a donation.

The other two people I was to get gifts for were the singer and the doorman. The singer leads in singing the sacred songs, while the doorman remains outside, tending the fire and opening and closing the front, and sometimes the rear flap. I was to give each of these a small present after each sweat, for the singer a bag of Bull Durham rolling tobacco, and for the doorman, who would probably be Chris, Gunter's teenage son, a notebook, or a pen. I was also to get a yards length each of five colors of cloth. I knew that these five pieces of white, red, blue, yellow, and green cloth were to be my "flags" and would hand from the ceiling of the sweat lodge during my four day sweat.

By tradition I had to supply a minimum of four kinds of food. At the end of every sweat everybody is supposed to consume some of each. The minimum meal consists of soup with meat and vegetables, bread, fruit, and coffee. Most of the meals are well-rounded with much more than just this minimum and so was the one we planned. Although I did do the shopping, it was a list dictated by Edie. I got the coffee and bread and four cans of sweet fruit, blueberries and cherries.

I got chicken and beef, five pounds of potatoes, various carrots, onions, etc. for the huge pot of soup which Edie made. I got fruit juice in concentrate and a big macaroni salad from a local restaurant, and Maria volunteered a dish each day. April and Donna also pitched in and by Friday afternoon I and the " family" that stood behind me were ready. Bill was going to help me get the firewood and would help tend the fire before the sweat. Finally it seemed like all the bases were covered, and it was time to begin.

The Four Day Healing Sweat lodge

Afternoon was becoming twilight as I took turns tending the fire with E.R. and Bill. Everything was done with obvious intent and purpose. Anytime a rock or piece of wood fell away from the eight and ten foot flames, one of us would quickly move forward with a shovel or pitchfork and return it to the fire. Coals and embers were meticulously returned to the fire, keeping its perimeter spotless. The intensity of the heat was increased because the fire was built inside a squarely u-shaped rock firewall, with the open end on the west facing the sweat lodge. The fire walls were about human height, with one side of the U extending to become the wood framed, plywood and corrugated roofing material wall that divided the sweat area from the driveway. There were wooden benches next to the dividing wall, where women in nightgowns and men in shorts, with towels draped over their shoulders, sat, watched, and waited.

I did not want to gawk or stare as E.R. went about his preparations before the sweat, but I didn't want to miss a thing. He had begun by bringing out a suitcase constructed of tin or aluminum that reminded me of cases made to carry musical instruments.

Inside were wings of an eagle, with cloth handles where the wing would have fit into the eagle's shoulder. There were buckskin patches filled with herbs, and other pouches. He moved about going back and forth to one of three areas, involved in ritual preparation and prayer.

I watched the others for behavioral clues and gathered that although E.R. was absorbed in what he was doing, it did not demand the silence or constant attention of others. In fact, those without specific fire watching responsibilities could be seen going back and forth, putting food up in the community room, going to change, or going to the outhouse. I watched E.R. as he prayed and tossed herbs and Sweetgrass on the blazing fire.

He took what I heard Eve call a "punk" of Sweetgrass, and as it burned like incense, purified the sweat lodge, the pipe mound in front of the sweat lodge, and the fire.

He carried objects from his case into the sweat lodge. He also carried in the five pieces of cloth that were my flags, they were to hang from the ceiling, in the west. He carried in his wings and other objects that I couldn't discern.

People did become quiet as E.R. obviously stood praying, while filling his pipe and preparing the pipe mound. This small mound is less than a foot high, a rounded area on which is placed the sacred pipe, nestled on top of a bunch of sage.

The mound is three or four feet from the front flap of the sweat lodge. I could see , besides the bed of sage and E.R.'s sacred pipe, a buckskin pouch decorated with beadwork, pouches of tobacco and envelopes containing gifts, and bunches of loose sage.

E.R. concluded his preparations and announced that it was time to go in. As we waited in line to go in I thought about how new this was to me. This sweat lodge looked like the Sioux ones I had read about, except the circular dome was covered with canvas and an old blue parachute, instead of the hides of deer and buffalo.

Those books seemed so far away, and I tried to remember what Eve and Edie had told me in preparation. I had remembered what they said concerning jewelry, either take it off or show it to E.R. and get him to cense it. They told me to pick up a few branches of sage and carry them in, placing a sprig behind the left ear for protection.

I watched E.R. bend double and touch his hands to the earth and rub them together, before entering the sweat lodge. We approached from the southern side and I remembered the warnings not to cut off the head of the turtle. The turtle is the sweat lodge, the turtles head is the pipe mound, and the imaginary neck is not to be crossed over. We would enter from the south, move clockwise around the sweat, and leave towards the north.

E.R. went in, circled the pit, and took his place by the door. Because it was a healing sweat for me, I was next. I did not overtly concern myself with the initial blessing of touching the earth and rubbing hands. I just got out of my wheelchair and crawled through the entrance, pausing but unable to rub my hands without losing balance. As I began the clockwise crawl around the fire pit I noticed that the texture of the ground was vastly different inside than in the immediate surrounding area. Whereas outside the ground was sandy the earth inside was hard packed, with some rocks visible where the earth had worn down around them. I tried to make a compromise between going slow enough to avoid dragging my knees and feet over the sharpest rocks, while trying to move faster than a snail.

E.R. was already lost unto himself and entered a world I could not see by the time I plunked down beside him, thankful for the soft Tule reeds we sat on. I looked around and could see what must be the twenty eight willow branches, tied together with string and vines, which comprised the structure to which was attached the canvas and old parachutes. The dome was probably four and a half 'feet in the middle, with a diameter between nine and twelve feet. From the branches over E.R.'s head I could see the eagle wings. In the back I could see my flags hanging down. In the middle the fire-pit was two feet deep and three feet across, a perfect circle cut flatly into the earth. The dirt walkway between the fire-pit and the Tule reeds was about a foot and a half wide, while the Tule reeds were adjacent to the walls everywhere except at the front flap. The Tule reeds were spread about two and a half feet wide and about three inches deep.

One by one people came in and took their places; each carried a bunch of sage, a towel, and had a sprig of sage behind their left ear. Eve had told me to chew sage if my mouth got too dry, and to hold it in front of my mouth, nose, or face if the steam felt too hot. She had assured me that although the steam might feel as though it were doing serious damage, she had never been hurt nor had she ever seen or heard of anybody being injured by participation in a sweat.

I noticed the seating arrangement, but was given no explanation for it. E.R. went in first and sat by the front flap. I was next, because I was the patient of the healing sweat. After I had settled in next to E.R., the women came in one by one and filled up the northern half of the circle. Then the men came one by one, taking their places, filling up the circle. The last man in would be the singer, and once he was settled E.R. called out to bring the rocks. A place next to the singer, an old Paiute named Paul, was left open, so Bill could help Gunter's son Chris bring the rocks quickly.

This was done quickly, quietly, efficiently, by the two men who alternately would bring one or two rocks on each pitchfork. Each rock, on the average, was larger than a softball, but not as big as a volley ball.

They appeared to me to be rocks of volcanic material, and they were red hot, with sparks of fire falling off when they collided. The pitchfork with the rocks would be set down right inside the front door, and with a quick motion the pitchfork was slid back leaving the rocks. E.R. would take each rock and place it in the fire-pit, placing them quickly and adeptly, using two forked sticks. These sticks were strong wood, cut from thick forked branches, and stripped clean of bark with a knife. They were about two feet long, and the wood was about an inch thick, the handle end was blunt, while the two tips of each branch came to a point.

The only sounds at this time were the noises of the rocks being brought and placed, and the grunts and groans of exertion made by those doing the bringing and placing. As I watched E.R. place the rocks I knew he was doing this in an intentional order, with symbolic meaning. The first four stones were placed in the four corners of the fire-pit, I assumed for the four Powers, the four directions. The next was placed in the center of the circle, for the Great Spirit, the Great Holy, the One from whom comes all four Powers, that exists in all that is. The next rock was placed beside the one in the middle, bringing the number to six. Eve had taught me that six in the Paiute system meant the four Powers, Mother Earth, and the Great Spirit as Grandfather Sky, or Those Above.

The rocks continued to come at a rapid rate until the pile was high over the rim of the fire-pit, a small mountain made of flaming and smoldering rock. When the last rock had been brought and placed, Bill asked for permission to come inside. E.R. grunted in approval and Bill came in and took his place next to Paul.

E.R. took one of his forked sticks and drew a geometrical design in the dirt between him and the fire. He called to Chris to bring the water and Chris brought a metal water bucket, filled with water, with a water ladle inside. E.R. took the bucket and lifted it high, by the handle and touched the bottom of the water pail to the top of the rocks, and held it for a second. He then placed the pail on top of the design he had just drawn.

E.R. called out to Chris to let the flap down and close it up. I saw the first furl of canvas come down from the roof and lay on the ground. It was arranged and I heard the second furl come down and get smoothed in place. Once the canvas had darkened the sides and been smoothed on the ground a long board put on top to keep it in place, and a few rocks were placed on top of the board. Chris asked E.R. if everything was O.K., E.R. grunted yes and we were secure in the darkness, the only light coming from the flickering and glowing rocks.

Chris was Gunter's younger son and had decided on his own to wait a few years before going in the sweat, he was fifteen or sixteen at the time. He often would be the doorman, he would watch the fire as it burned out, and open the front and sometimes the back flaps as E.R.

commanded.

As we sat there in the darkness, sweat began to pour from every part of my body. I had strange thoughts then, not really serious, but I thought for the first time how truly vulnerable I was. Because of all the secrecy, no one but those there knew where I was. Except for Eve's visit to Georgia, I had known everyone there for less than two full weeks. What if I was a bad judge of character? I thought about the Manson family and other insane people, bizarre cults. What if I had been fooled, and these people were into Satan worship or human sacrifice. Doesn't evil usually hide behind the face of goodness? Someone could club me or stab me easily in the darkness, and there were a million ways to dispose of a body on a lightly populated desert reservation. Didn't people die or go to jail every day because of poor judgment? My panic reached its' apex at this point of logic, and then subsided. As much as I could judge anything, I felt certain that no such evil lurked in the hearts of people like Eve, and

Edie, and Donna and so I calmed down and became rational again.

E.R. began talking and I remembered why I was there and what I hoped for. E.R. began talking and it was a statement of intent, and although everyone knew some of the things he said, it was as though he needed to say them in the sweat lodge during ritual. He said that this was the first round of a four day sweat for me, and he would refer to me by name, or more often as "my friend here. He said that I had come a long way and that we were all going to do what we could for me. E.R. said something to the effect of, "Now, if anybody else needs help for anything, now is the time to speak up. You can pray for yourselves, your families, and my friend here, but that's all. And if any of you have spirits or a relative who has passed on who could help, you can ask them to help - to help so that things can be good, for you and your relations. Pray to the heavenly father, pray to Jesus if you want, but pray hard, cry out. If you cry out from the heart, maybe the Great Spirit has pity on you, and spirits come, so that things can be good."

Paul's wife Lilly was the first at this point to use the formula, " E.R. may I speak." E.R. grunted yes and Lilly mentioned a sick relative and asked everyone to pray for her.

Then Eve asked for and was given permission to speak and began by thanking E.R. for the sweat, thanked the Great Spirit for E.R. and his sweat lodge, and thanked the Great Spirit for my coming and for this healing opportunity. After that it was as though she my teacher was introducing me to the sweat lodge, saying a little about me, mentioning the group in Atlanta and that I had already begun healing. I was embarrassed but proud at the same time, and when she was through E.R. announced that the first few days would be for cleansing, and the last two for healing. He took the water ladle and began pouring dipper-fills of water on the top of the rock and people broke into spontaneous praying as the steam hissed and filled the air. I could hear an occasional "Ho! -

the word always used instead of the English word yes or to show strong approval.

I joined in the praying, stating as Eve had told me to, my needs and desire for healing, and praying for those there, and for Lilly's relative. These prayers are spoken out loud, but at the same time they are private. Before the singing these prayers are almost murmured, but while the singing is going on, anyone at any time may revert back to this spontaneous prayer, which may become louder, even to the point of yelling out.

E.R. and Paul began singing, and others immediately joined in. Paiute singing is slow and lilting and majestic and can convey the full range of human emotion. It is much slower than the fast paced, staccato drumming music of the Great Plains tribes, which is the style of native music the Average American has been exposed to via Hollywood and the war dance. I had gone through some circular conversations with Eve and Edie about the singing. They had told me it was important for me to show respect for the Indian Way, and to sing out loud and enthusiastically, despite my protestations that my voice was not the envy of sparrows. They had told me that these songs were to the fire and the rocks and the spirits whose help was wanted. Eve explained that the songs at the appropriate time implored, invoked, greeted, served as a vehicle for the power of, and said thanks and goodbye to the spirits who did the healing. When I asked if they could teach me some of the words they said no. Eve had laughed and said for years she went to sweat, and knew every song inside, and forgot them all as soon as she went outside. When I asked if she could tell me what the songs said. She said no, that while some of the songs are made up of real words in Paiute, that other songs were just combinations of sounds that made up a song, no words or meanings, just a mantra of melodious sounds used to contact a certain spirit. While some of these songs have been passed down unknown generations, songs are constantly created as new people develop relationships with a spirit and receive from that spirit - in fast or prayer - the spirit song to call it. Eve had reassured me that if I just joined in; it would come naturally to me, and to an unexpected degree what she said was true.

These songs involve a great deal of repetition, they are not long and the same song may be sung for fifteen minutes. The Paiute language, however, seems to have a tendency to use consonants at the beginnings of words in a manner not common to English, and there were some words I couldn't figure out even when just listening and not singing along. The amazing thing to me was the way the same song could change in tone and feeling while being sung. So I joined in the singing and sporadically would revert to prayer, trying as E.R. had told me, to cry out from the heart.

This was a kind of heat I had never experienced before, in a life filled with sports played in the southern heat. The hot steam was everywhere; sweat was pouring, and I made the mistake of trying to take a deep breath through my mouth. My throat and mouth were scorched and I used my sage, chewing a little and holding some against my face. Eve had told me that of the four rounds, the first was to invoke and implore, the second to greet the spirits, and begin working, the third round is the working round and the fourth is to thank the spirits and to say farewell. The first round seemed awful hot and long, and I hoped I could take it. Finally the singing ended, there were Ho!s shouted, and E.R. called out to Chris to open the front.

One of the women asked E.R. if he would open the back flap to and he grunted and called out to Chris to open the back up too. As the front opened and cool air rushed in I looked around to find everyone drenched and slumping, or leaning back against the wall of the lodge. The back opened and after a minute or two people started using their towels and sitting up more. Whether water is available between rounds, and whether the back flap will be raised or left down is entirely up to the shaman. Eve told me that during some four day healing sweats there was no water between rounds, but there was no hardcore rule.

After five minutes of silence E.R. told Chris to close up, which he did in reverse order closing the back first. Once we were sealed in E.R. said that this was the second round and began pouring dipperful's of water on the rocks. People began praying and the singing began shortly. Whereas the first round`s songs had been the painful and sad call for help from the suffering, the second round`s songs were a happier greeting, more hopeful and optimistic, and towards the end of the second round, they carried strength.

I had never been so hot or sweated so much in so short a time. I and the others had continued to sing and pray and finally E.R. cried Ho! Everyone cried Ho! In response, and he issued orders to Chris to open them both up.

I was being supported by one of the willow poles as I leaned back, and I saw that others were doing the same or else were lying down around each other, leaning towards the cool breeze. E.R. lay with his head at the front door, with his eyes closed. I remembered how during my preparation Eve had warned me that it was always worse much harder and more difficult for the medicine man and the patient than anyone else. E.R. had gotten up and moved around during the singing, which would have taken him closer to the rocks, and higher up, where the hottest steam was.

After we had cooled down for a few minutes and people had used their towels and begun to sit up, E.R. began to talk. Eve had told me that in sweat we would pray in English, sing in Paiute, and when E.R. talked between rounds everyone would speak English.

E.R. told me that I had to really cry out, that I had to beg the Heavenly Father for help, that He might take pity on me and heal me. He explained in no uncertain terms that since the whole thing was for me that

I had to do my part which was really cry out, to beg and plead. How could I expect help if I wasn't willing to really ask for it? I nodded my head and said Ho! Eve had explained that the shaman had absolute authority in the sweat lodge, his word was law. She said that our submission to his authority symbolized the submission of our personal will to the authority of the Great Spirit, an expression of the attitude - not my, but Thy will be done.

The flaps were closed, the water poured, the songs begun, and I tried to cry out more. I was not surprised at what he said because I had experienced inner conflict every time the word "beg" had been included in my instructions. I had been brought up to think that pride to the point of arrogance was wrong, but I had also been raised thinking that pride in yourself and self-respect were important and desirable qualities. There was a vast gulf in my mind between both the connotation and denotation of the word "ask" from the word "beg." I could ask for something, whether

I deserved it or not, but I had never begged from God or man, with one justifiable exception.

I had asked once at a hospital; immediately after the worst accident of my life, if they could give me a drug to kill a pain worse than I had ever known or imagined. They said no. I begged. They said no – internal bleeding. So I tried to beg for the second time in my life, and I tried to really cry out from my heart.

I cried out to my Creator and I said that I wanted to be well and whole again. I confessed my multitudinous sins, and I asked to be healed anyway. I told how tired I was of pain, and frustration, and limitation, and that I wanted to be the way I was born again, whole and well, that I wanted to enjoy the simple pleasure of running, of walking barefoot in the grass, of being free, free to enjoy Nature and life without the limitation of a wheelchair, without being stared at everywhere I go. I called out from my heart and released anger, frustration, expressed my desires and hopes, I screamed out loud, as loud as I could - "O God Help Me! Heal Me!" and felt the salt of my tears join the sweat on my face.

I sang the songs, cried out for help, and absolutely could not believe the heat. E.R. got up and worked on me while I was singing and praying. The two things I remember clearly were being sprayed with water and being cleaned out. He spayed me with water - I presume by drinking a mouthful and spraying it on my head. To someone not familiar with shamanic practice, it might seem strange, but I understood that the water had become sacred through ritual consecration, and was being sprayed on my head to cleanse and purify me. This caught me by surprise but certainly did not offend me, and was actually refreshing. When I say he cleaned me out it is for lack of a better term. He took his hands and ran them down my body with a strong pulling motion. He did this front and back, and I felt like: he was pulling the bad, the evil, the negativity out of me, and then throwing it in the fire, to be transformed.

Finally, after what seemed an incredibly long time the songs were ended, the "Ho!s" were shouted, the flaps were open, and not one human being was still sitting. Bodies, mine included, were laying limp, spread all over the Tule reeds and the bare dirt floor. There were some small movements towards the cool air flowing in and eventually people even sat up and used there already soaked towels. E.R. announced that we could have water and one by one, in no definite order we went through the formula, "E.R. may I have water`,` the Paiutes use their word for water, paiha. E.R. would then take the water ladle and fill it in the bucket and pass it clockwise around the circle.

Each person takes the ladle and passes it to the person next to them. When it gets to the person who asked for it, they will take the ladle and make a sacrifice before drinking. This is usually done by holding the ladle up and over the rocks, and pouring a little out for the Great Spirit, the earth Mother, and the spirits who have helped. After pouring once on the rocks, a trail of water is often laid leading from the rocks to the person. They then drink and pour the cool water on their head and body. They then pass the ladle to the person next to them and so on until it finishes the clockwise circle back to E.R.

When everyone had gotten water E.R. told us that it was the fourth round coming up and to clean up in front of us. This meant to clean the dirt area directly in front of us, to pull any loose Tule reeds back where they belong and scrape any small pieces of Tule back with a straight reed. Once this was done the flaps came down and the final round began. The singing of this round was not the strong, powerful singing of the third working round; this was lighter, saying thanks and goodbye. When E.R. poured the last of the water on the rocks, the last song was brought to a close, the HO!s sounded, murmurs of thank-you, and thank-you Grandfathers were said, and the flaps were opened. E.R. had placed the water pail on top of the rocks and was lying towards the door, and again there were bodies lying everywhere.

Again as the cool reviving air poured in, people sat up, dried off, cleaned up in front, and gathered together the sage they had brought in. E.R. talked a little bit and told me that I had done much better the third and fourth rounds, that I had done o.k. He told me that I had a bad temper and that I should try not to lose my temper in general and specifically while I was being purified and healed. He told me to watch out, that I'd be tempted.

E.R finished talking and told Chris to bring the Sacred Pipe. Chris took the pipe off the pipe-mound and brought it to the door. Paul rubbed his hands on the bare earth and then rubbed them together to receive the pipe in a sacred manner. He took the pipe as Chris handed it to him, and holding the bowl in his left hand, drew a clockwise circle in the air with the pipe stem. He took out the plug of sage E.R. had put in after filling the pipe earlier at the pipe-mound. He touched the bowl to the ground and lit the pipe. He smoked and blew out to the six directions, the Great Spirit above, the Mother Earth below, and the four powers of the four directions. He smoked for a while, eyes closed and the passed the pipe on in circular fashion, clockwise.

Each person took the pipe and smoked it in a ritual fashion, but not everyone did the same thing. Everybody touched their hands to the earth and rubbed them before receiving the pipe. Not everyone would hold the bowl and make a circle with the stem. Some people would smoke with the bowl resting on the ground throughout the time they smoked. Others would touch the ground and then hold the pipe while smoking. Some blew the smoke out to the four directions while others took an exhalation of smoke and with their hands would rub smoke on the four sides of their body. This was done either front-back, side-side, or was done front-right-back-left in a clockwise style. Despite the obvious variations, everyone treated the pipe with the utmost respect, touched it to the earth before smoking, and acknowledged the six powers/directions before turning their attention inward to their prayers.

The smoking time is silent, and people do not look around or make eye contact. It is the time for silent prayer and communion with the Great Spirit and the Earth Mother.

I had read the Sacred Pipe and talked with Eve enough to understand why the pipe must be touched to the ground and the six direction/powers acknowledged. I recalled how the white Buffalo Cow Woman had brought the Sioux the Sacred Pipe and told them it was Holy and would take them unto the end. She had told them that the Earth was sacred and that every step taken upon her should be a prayer. She showed them the bowl was red stone, that it was of the Earth and that the stem was wood and represented everything that lives upon the Earth. I knew that when E.R. had filled his pipe earlier at the pipe-mound that the first pinch of tobacco was for the Great Spirit and that the second pinch was for the Earth Mother, the next for the power of the East, the fourth for the South, the fifth for the West, then for the North. After the six were included in his pipe, then all living creatures were included, a 'pinch for the two legged, the four legged, a pinch for those that crawl, and for those that swim, a pinch for all the rocks - the entire mineral kingdom, all the plants-the vegetable kingdom, and pinches for the animal and human kingdoms.

E.R. would have put a pinch for each of the four elements; air, fire, water and earth, for Grandfather Sky and the Star Children, for all there is. He put in a pinch for each of his spirit powers and a pinch for all the spirits, and for all the Grandfathers, and a pinch for the Grandfathers of the region, whom he would have invited to smoke along with him. That when he smoked his pipe he would pray to the Great Spirit for everything, and that he would pray to the Great Spirit with everything. I had smoked with Eve every day and knew that she considered it very holy magic, and though she didn't like to use the word magic there was no other word that fit. We had discussed that the pipe was equivalent to the bread and wine of the Christian Eucharist and equivalent to the Magical Weapons of Pagan ritual - the sword which rules the element of fire, the wand which rules the element of air, the chalice which rules the element of water, and the pentacle which rules the element of earth. The Sacred Pipe combines so much symbolism, so simply. The smoker fills the bowl with everything, touches it to the earth and smokes, sending his prayers out as the smoke rises towards the heavens. Smoking magically combines all the elements in the act of prayer. The tobacco is of the earth, as is the bowl and stem. When fire is put in the bowl and air sucked through it, the resulting smoke enters the mouth and lungs and comes into contact with the water of saliva and the moisture of mucous membranes.

This inhaled smoke which has actively combined all four elements is then exhaled as the prayers are sent forward. I was very aware that pipestone is also fragile and can break if dropped as the pipe came my way. I didn't want to cough like some kid smoking his first cigarette, but the sweat had dried me out so badly I coughed some anyway. I kept the bowl on the ground as I went through the six powers and said silent thank-yous for being where I was in the situation I was, and passed the pipe to E.R.

I didn't smoke it very long, it was the first time I had smoked his pipe, and I was too self-conscious to get lost in prayer. The healer must finish smoking the pipe, and it seemed like he had to smoke it a long time to finish it, making me feel like I should have kept it and prayed longer.

When he was through he put away the matches and handed Chris the pipe to put back on the pipe-mound. E.R. gathered his towel and sage and went out. I was tired and a little shaky as I crawled out, very aware that I must not slip and fall on the rocks, and that once outside I must turn to the left and not cut off the turtle's head.

With my towel on my shoulders and what I could find of my sage temporarily between my teeth, I crawled out without mishap and Chris brought my chair around the turtles head as the others came out. I used every bit of strength I had left to perform the ground to chair transfer.

The night air was cool as I sat there for a few minutes, regaining my strength. Eve and Edie smiled and patted me on the shoulder and went with the women to change in the community room. I finally went out to my car, opened the door and changed there. My clothes were incredibly heavy from acquired sweat. I had already given E.R. his four presents, so I grabbed the notebook I had brought for Chris, and the tobacco I would give to Paul, and headed on to the ceremonial meal.

The community room is a cement block building, probably twice as long as it is wide. When I went in there were people sitting at the long table that runs the length of the dining area, and there were people milling about the kitchen, which took up about the northern 1/5 th of the building. The kitchen had a sink, with indoor plumbing, and there was an old refrigerator and stove.

There were two doors leading from the dining area to the kitchen, and the food was set out on the table in the kitchen, which was flush against the partition wall..

E.R. went through the kitchen and came out with a piece of bread on which was piled various foods. He walked to the head of the table and held up one hand and everybody became silent. He said grace in both English and Paiute, thanking the heavenly Father for all the blessings, for the food, for the people. As he finished, I heard a few simultaneous` amens. E.R. then carried the loaded bread outside. When he came back he told Chris to go ahead and go first, and a line of tired, thirsty, hungry people formed behind him.

I learned the Doorman always goes first, but there is no special order after that. There was more food than I expected, Edie had made sure I met the requirements, and Donna, April, and Maria had all pitched in. There was tea and fruit juice and coffee, all the foods I had mentioned, and salads and casseroles, and it looked like any other pot-luck affair. Eve had told me I had to eat the required four, the soup, bread, fruit, and coffee, and that I should try to eat some of everything, so that like anywhere else, no chef's feelings were hurt.

People talked while they ate and the conversation varied from normal - where are you from, what do you do - to talking about how good the food was - to talking about the weather - to talking about the sweat we had just gone through. There seemed little social distance between the Anglos and the Paiutes, I guessed that most of these people had known each other for years, I was the only outsider. I tried talking to Paul and Lilly and received pleasant smiles, but our conversation was hindered by Paul's poor hearing. They were quite elderly, yet seemed very alert and mobile.

Once most people were through eating, and just sat around digesting, the conversation seemed to take a more serious spiritual turn. It seemed like some would ask E.R. a question and when he began to answer, the peripheral conversations would cease and attention would become centered on his response. It was a very warm environment, the sweat seeming to increase both one's appetite and appreciation of food. When I asked E.R. how many four days sweats did it take for the curing of a serious injury such as mine, he said he didn't know. Sometimes one four day was all that was needed, sometimes it took several.

Conversation didn't seem to last very long, people began putting food away for tomorrow, cleaning empty dishes, and leaving one by one. People seemed happy, tired, and content, and the good-byes were verbally affectionate.

We made the fifty-seven mile drive home with one down, three to go. I bathed and went to bed as was suggested. In my journal and in a letter to Peggy

I recorded my impressions. I described the sweat saying, "it is very high, very powerful, and a tremendous ordeal/hardship." I also recorded what Eve had considered a good omen for the sweats.

That morning, while smoking her pipe, she had seen a golden eagle, followed by four crows. That night I felt exhausted on many levels, and quickly fell asleep.

I slept twelve hours that night and by the time I got going it was time to go to sweat. The second and third sweats were afternoon sweats, and the fourth was another night sweat. On the drive up a single crow flew across the road, low, not far above my windshield. A little later I saw three hawks flying together, and before I reached the reservation, I saw another single hawk. Eve had told me to watch the birds and take note..

The preparations went the same as before, but I had a prior determination to do a better job of calling out. E.R. had told me to go about it like the night before, the same way he had Eve years before.

He told me that if I wanted this healing I had to send up a squawk, and keep sending up a squawk for help, and that help could come if for no other reason than to shut me up. It was a funny image but he was telling me if I asked sincerely enough, persistently enough, an answer, hopefully healing, would come.

The daylight sweat lodge was full of different sensation than the sweat at night.. This was the second and final day of purification and as soon as he began pouring water on the rocks and the spontaneous praying broke out I was aware that I was *less* concerned with how big a fool I might be, or if I was so loud others might hear me, than I was concerned that I was going to cry out from the heart and really ask for what I really wanted most. The songs were easier to sing, the words easier to pronounce and I was able to express my emotions while singing. It was incredibly hot, and the relentless rhythm of the songs, the outpouring of emotion while singing, the spontaneous praying, asking, begging, confessing, had me entering an altered state, and cleansing and opening my heart, providing me with immense catharsis. To aid this inner cleansing, this inner process of purification, there is the leadership of the shaman and the support system of the other participants, and there is a strong symbolic suggestion given by the sweat lodge itself, that of entering a womb and that of leaving a womb. I also had hope, and had the feeling that I was sacrificing and working hard for my healing.

At the end of the second and third rounds, after the flaps were opened and people had cooled off and sat back up, E.R. and others commented on the coming of what E.R. called animal spirits and doctoring spirits. These spirits were of various origins, the shaman is expected to have at least one, and more commonly three or more animal spirits. He may also have relationships with many more spirits that belong to other medicine men in his "craft network," spirits of medicine men he works with and goes through ritual with, spirits he has been given the right to call by those medicine men. The spirits that come may have relationships with others in the sweat, Eve and Paul I know had spirits, and probably others. Spirits may be sent by the regional Grandfathers, or even the archetypal Grandfather Animal spirits. These spirit powers are usually obtained through a vision or dream while fasting, or through a dream in normal sleeping, sometimes they are inherited or transferred, but this is much rarer. In previous discussions I have mentioned those spirits found in works by Eve and anthropologist Julian Steward forming a list among which are bat, bear, buffalo, coyote, eagle, fox, and wolf, and two phenomenon of nature, one specific mountain, the other, being the blue haze over the valley. My experience that day and for years to come would include those animal spirits other than the bat and fox, and would include only one phenomenon of nature, that as a spirit power acted as a bridge for the other spirits to traverse.

I have mentioned that of the elementals, my experience did not include water babies or giants. I am hesitant to list previously unlisted animal spirits, as I am to relate any specific spirit to any living person, because it might not be in accord with the promises I made, and it might be offensive to shaman involved.

The presence and activities of these spirits was reported by E.R. as he worked, and also during the breaks between rounds which is when others would relate their impressions and perceptions. E.R.'s work was done in association with his animal spirits. They would tell him what to do and how to doctor; or he would experience a unity with them where he might behave like that animal and it would guide his behavior; he might direct them into the body of a patient or direct them to heal at a distance. In unity of consciousness he might "astrally project" in the form of his animal spirit. The shaman is expected to know when the spirits come, to see them, talk with them, work with them, but he is not expected to be omnipotent and every participant is expected to report on any spiritual manifestation. The shaman is not expected to see every spirit that comes, but he is the ultimate and final authority on how to interpret what happens in sweat.

When people go through the formula to obtain permission to speak and tell E.R. what they have perceived, it most often happens that they have seen or heard something internally, in their mind, Sometimes people reported seeing points of light moving around the lodge, other might feel the presence of a spirit as Eve did, feeling talons or something similar. Sometimes people would see a spirit in its` animal form, internally, or seemingly externally. When someone would report a spirit, E.R. would usually ask that person to challenge the spirit by asking it if it was good, if it was there to help. Then the person would hold an internal dialogue and report the answer back, and I have no recollection of this process ever ending in a negative judgment.

My journal records that there were six animal spirits reported present that day. They were of two of the species mentioned, plus a small, almost insect size bird sent to do intricate work inside the body. E.R. seemed as surprised as I was when he announced that one of his animal spirits had brought a friend, an animal spirit of the same species. He told me that this animal spirit was like his, except that it was for me. He told me that the Grandfather animal spirit sent it and I was to pray to that Grandfather, that he would help me. At the time I was totally unprepared to realize the importance and significance of this event within the context of the originating culture.

At the end of the third round E.R. announced that the purifying was over and that the healing would begin. The sweat had been extremely hot and I had put my heart and soul into my squawking. To cleanse me he had worked with his hands, sprayed me with water, given me an unidentified herb to chew, and sucked on the top of my forehead. To heal he would put his spirits into my body, he would work on me with his hands, and he would beat around me and on me with his eagle feathers. By the end of the fourth round, when people had managed to sit back up and we had smoked the pipe, I became aware of a pulsating with in my hands and feet. This was a feeling of excess energy not unlike that reported from strong doses of amphetamines or cocaine. This pulsating was accompanied by a tingling, buzzing sensation. When it was time to crawl out I became aware of how tired and weak I had become. I could barely manage to crawl and did so far enough to get outside and fall away from the turtle's neck and out of the way of the others. I stayed and rested, trying to regain my strength.

As I crawled out I was deeply aware of the feeling that I had been purged clean, that I had been reborn.

The ceremonial meal went as it had the day before, and after the meal E.R. talked to me privately about my animal spirit. He told me to pray to the Grandfather of which my animal spirit was a representative and to treat it as a friend, it could not be commanded but it would help me if I asked it for help. He told me to pray often with tobacco or food. I would pray with tobacco either by leaving some for my spirit in a place of nature, or I could smoke tobacco in a sacred manner and invite the spirit to smoke with me. I would do this with a hand rolled cigarette or a normal pipe, by taking the first six inhalations for the six direction/powers and the seventh for the Grandfather animal spirit. To pray with food I would do as E.R. did before the meal, pray and take the food offering outside.

I asked what kind of food should I feed my spirit, and was told it would eat whatever I did. He told me not to worry what physical creatures ate the offering, that the spirit would receive the energy of it.

I had noticed since being with Eve, foregoing alcohol and all intoxicants, I now remembered all my dreams, or at least four to six more dreams a night than normal. I considered many of these dreams to be mechanisms for psychological venting, containing many images of violence, and of people consuming alcohol and drugs, and of debauchery in general. I considered this dream hyper-activity to be a cleansing of my sub-conscious, as the sweats were cleaning my mind and soul. The dreams that I considered as the worst temptation to lose the positive state of mind I was attempting to maintain were dreams of an intimate personal nature depicting scenes of deceit and betrayal.

At the time I considered these dreams to be the predicted temptation, months later I was unhappily astounded when they turned out to be totally accurate. Like the night before, I was exhausted on all levels, and slept twelve hours.

Sunday's preparations were the same as the two days before, but the number of people waiting to sweat was increased by a Paiute family of four, the couple was in their early forties, their daughters in their early twenties. I was to see in the next two years an attendance pattern I noticed during that first series, basically attendance was a family affair, either elderly or middle aged couples post-puberty yet unmarried female relatives. Occasionally a lone middle aged or elderly man would appear, but I saw no young Indian men, and few married couples on the younger side of middle aged. The Anglo attendance was primarily young couples, and the lone young male was not uncommon. Eve had told me that although E.R. longed for young men in the valley to come forward and take interest, no young Paiute were forthcoming. Eve told me that E.R. had raised ten children yet none of his sons expressed interest in shamanism. One of his sons had even referred to his father's shamanic work as superstitious hocus-pocus. From my own observations over the next two years the Paiute youth of the valley seemed every bit as lost and seduced by the sex-drugs-and-rock-and-roll philosophy as was the mainstream American youth of the time.

The sweat proceeded as the other two, with the main difference being in the statement of intent, that this was my first full doctoring healing sweat. The family of Paiutes had a life situation in need of healing and everyone prayed for them, too. The main difference observables between sweats were which songs, in which order, would be sung, and which spirits would be invited, and which spirits would appear.

Before the second and third rounds E.R. would often state the various spirits he was inviting in starting with a generalized invitation to the spirits of the mountains and the spirits of the valley. This could include but was not limited to the old men-little men of the mountains but seemed to indicate that animal spirits lived in and watched over certain areas of the valley and adjacent mountains. Then he would invite the Grandfather animal spirits, expecting his own animal spirits as their intermediaries. He might also ask certain of his relatives who have passed away to help.

I was glad that Sunday to see more Paiutes than Anglos; it

somehow made the whole process seem more legitimate. The rocks seemed unbearably hot, and it looked as if more were added because of more sweaters .From the very beginning the singing was strong and powerful.

Early in the first round while I was singing with my eyes closed, a white form took shape against my black field of vision. I concentrated my attention on this form and although I expected it to dissolve, it remained while I looked at and pondered it, for over ten seconds, but less than thirty. It reminded me of a revolver turned upside down, a white image of the handle and the trigger guard. It occurred to me that it might be an oddly shaped pipe, and I made the mental note to ask Eve later.

The second and third rounds were hot and the singing was very strong. Between rounds E.R. commented on how many spirits were showing up at the same time. Over three species were represented, but he didn`t say exactly how many individual spirits there were. I also noted that Paiute women sometimes sing in a certain way that the Anglos can't or won't. This is similar to a sound South American women make, a tremelo that vibrates the sound of the voice. Paiute men and Anglo men sound the same, however.

During the singing of the third round I verbally subordinated my will to the Will of the Great Spirit. When Eve had suggested such an affirmation was needed for my spiritual development yet a part of my mind had remained resistant.

She had observed that it was my strength of will that took me through the process of rehabilitation and the relentless pain filled nights, but that I ran the risk of nurturing my personal will in lieu of submission to Divine Will. I had argued that being made in the image of Cod the creator, it was our duty to likewise create with our own will. I said that I was sick of hearing people talking about "going with the flow" or that no matter what they did or didn't do, "whatever happens is the Lord's will".

I had also had trouble in general with the thought that the ultimate Mother-Father Creator of all Life had my best possible life already planned and was waiting anxiously to reveal it. I told her if God told me what to do, I would do it, but until then I had to trust my intuition. She countered that that was her point, to listen to one's highest intuition instead of just one's personal desire and will. I had no problem with that logic and so concurred. When I reported my affirmation of `Thy Will be done` to Eve and E.R. later at the ceremonial meal I got two distinctly different reactions for the first time. Eve was happy and thought I had taken an important step. E.R. seemed barely concerned and told me not to be so concerned with the mind and thoughts, but with the experience. He said the important thing was to ask from the heart.

The heat was as devastating as before, while E.R. worked on me during the second and third rounds. Sometimes I would sit up and sing and other times he had me lay down, he did some of the things he had done earlier, but mainly he manipulated me with his hands and worked around and on me with the eagle fans that felt as if they had been held over the rising steam. I gathered from what E.R. and others had said during breaks there were many spirits present and working and that everyone considered it a powerful sweat. I felt as exhausted at the ends of the rounds, and people were lying about as before when the flaps were opened, yet I seemed to recover quicker during the breaks than the previous sweats..

The thank-you songs of the fourth round were enthusiastic and when we had blessed ourselves and the flaps had been opened, I sat up quicker than previously, and felt comfortable later when it was my turn to smoke the Sacred Pipe. The ritual and meal continued to have the same form, but that day I noticed something that I was to observe at later sweats. The social distance that had existed between the Paiutes and Anglos who didn't know each other before had disappeared during the sweat but reappeared during the ceremonial meal, to a lessened extent, however.

That night before Eve's weekly group met I showed Eve a picture of the shape I had seen in the first round. She said it was definitely a pipe and not a revolver handle upside down. She said that her Indian ancestors, whom she referred to at the time as Micmac, used pipes that were carved in that shape, She said I could tell E.R. about the vision and I could even ask him for a Sacred Pipe, but that I could only ask him once. She went on to say that it was a common occurrence for anyone who became interested in Native American spiritual practices to want a pipe. She knew of Indians who had waited years for one. She also mentioned E.R. carved a Plains Indian style pipe and to her knowledge only carved them in that style.

I told her I would probably mention it to E.R. but that I knew not to have great expectations. After the weekly class was over I was so tired

I couldn't stay awake to write, and drifted off to sleep.

The last sweat followed the course the previous three. My attitude before beginning the sweat was slightly ambivalent. In my wildest and most optimistic moments I had hoped to be running fifty yard dashes by the fourth day, or at least noticed some physiological improvement, yet Eve and E.R. had both told me that healing would be spiritual and purifying before it was physical, and that many four day sweats could be required. The previous day's sweat had felt powerful and though I hadn't experienced the spirits I had heard about, I had experienced the unsolicited upside-down revolver-pipe image. The day's sweat was to remedy my lack of perception of the spirits and their power, as it was to challenge my preconceptions about the interplay between physical reality and perception of it, as surely as it was forever etched upon my memory.

I have mentioned that the spirit songs conveyed different feeling at different times, were used to implore and plead in the first round, and to thank and wish farewell in the last round, and during the second and third rounds were what Eve called receiving songs. By this I understood her to mean that during the working rounds which are the second and third, the songs are offered up to receive the energy of the spirits. That the healing energy that was directed through the spirits, blends itself and works through the physical sound which permeates the sweat lodge and the people within. During the second and third rounds is when the singing is most adamant, the shaman as a healer is most active, altered states most deeply entered into, and the presence and associated phenomenon of the spirits most noted.

The second and third round of the last day provided me with a whole new insight concerning shamanism and spirit power. The sweat was very hot and the singing very strong. I was very tired from the previous three, and my lips were chapping and cracking.

Both knees, and toes on both feet were scraped and cut from the process of crawling in. I had received permission after the second sweat to wear socks and blue jeans, rolled up with doubled cloth over my knees, in to sweat. They made things that much hotter. My skin was dried out and felt like leather. Eve had stressed tome that a sweat was sacrifice, and I took the dehydration process in stride, I hoped, as part of the sacrifice for healing.

E.R. would work on me during the second and third rounds, but that did not consume all the time. I would sit and sing unless he indicated, either by touch or abbreviated speech, that he wanted me to lie down. Once when he had me lying face down on the Tule reeds he pressed his eagle fan against my bare back and held it. I did not resist, but was certain from the heat of the fan, which must have been held over the steam, that I was burned, that I would find a blister or tender red skin where the fan had been. It hurt and it felt that hot. The pain, however went away quickly, and later I found no marks or indications of a burn.

As was the case the day before E.R. and others reported the presence of many spirits. There were as many as six species of animal spirits some of which were represented by more than just an individual. Eve had written about the Thunderbird Eagle - Thunderbird Man as being of a different nature than the Grandfather animal spirits and my experience that day and later led me to concur.

The Thunderbird Eagle-Thunderbird Man is invoked and treated as a great Power, and I conceived of it as a demi-urge, and by analogy, similar to the Hindu Vac or the Christian Logos, representing in the symbol of thunder the creative aspect of the Word of God.

Eve later told me that it would probably be best not to tell too many people about the kind of manifestations that can occur during a sweat, unless I was interested on being sent for rest somewhere where the help would all be dressed in white. However my reading on shamanism since then has given me the assurance that my perceptions, and those of my `fellow sweaters` is not out of place in the cultural and cross-cultural context of shamanic folk-lore. Also as ethnography of ritual and change of ritual the associated phenomenon must be reported as a valid part of the study, so I must apologize to those this may offend and tell the story.

Obviously the combined effects of the inherent symbolism within a sweat lodge ritual, and the praying, confessing, pleading, begging, the emotive and repetitious singing of the spirit songs, the strong leadership of the shaman, the concern and support of the participants, and the shared sweating and heat exhaustion, all produce within the participants a change in consciousness, an altered state. Yet this altered state of consciousness is not the deeply relaxed waking-sleep of hypnosis. Because there is no light the other senses may become more aware, especially the awareness of sound in hearing the singing of oneself and others. The shared concern and sacrifice and religious devotion can lead into that previously mentioned state of well-being, where one may feel more strongly than normal a faith in spiritual realities and a generalized feeling of love for creation and the created. Although the participants may enter an altered state it is of course individual and would vary as much as the lives of the participants vary. Even though there are expectations of phenomenon; the reported manifestations are specific in content and verbal revelation.

People may see, hear, and feel things, but these experiences are not the free, uncontrolled, kaleidoscopic hallucinations of LSD or similar hallucinogens. There is a conscious awareness of what is happening around oneself, as there is of one's internal dialogue. What one experience is, however, different in context and event than what one experiences during "the normal working world day."

Until the fourth sweat my unusual experiences were limited to the buzzing, tingling, pulsating of my hands and feet, and the pipe vision.

On the third day, either because it was a daytime sweat or I had been in long enough for my eyes to adjust, or both, I noticed something that I couldn`t explain, but could have been the result of natural causes. During one of the working rounds, it appeared that as E.R. poured water on the rocks, the steam came back enveloping us, and not dispersing in a general pattern. There may have been some way the wind outside effected the steam inside, through unobservable small cracks at the doors or pinprick holes in the canvas, or something physical. I did clearly observe the steam pouring towards shaman and patient, seemingly for the moment ignoring the others around the circle, focused on the main event.

By the end of the third sweat I had been given an animal spirit and experienced some odd perceptions, but had no direct contact or understanding of the spirits. The fourth sweat was extremely hot and I was very tired from the previous three. The songs were sung with force and the manifestations of spirits were reported early. I had two experiences, both in the third round. The first and easily explainable was that I heard a bear snort. It did not sound like a man imitating a bear, it sounded like a bear. This is a fairly common experience in folk-lore, hearing the sound an animal makes verbally, or while in natural movement. Eve would often hear the wings beating the air as a spirit came or went. This is also an easily fake-able phenomenon. The other phenomenon would be as difficult to fake as it is to explain. The phenomenon is associated with Grandfather Buffalo, although buffalo, if ever present in the valley, were never numerous. The connection with buffalo, I gathered from later conversations, had come about because one of the teachers Eve and E.R. shared was an Arapaho Buffalo healer. Grandfather Buffalo, probably because he wasn't native to the area, was one of the least invoked of the animal spirits already mentioned. If he was invoked that third round, unless it was by a song in Paiute that was begun without prior mention, it was in a group of animal spirits without special mention.

However when the phenomenon discussed was over, E.R. thanked Grandfather Buffalo for his appearance, for his healing, and for his blessing at the end of the round.

I can only describe my own experience although I asked four of the Anglos, individually, at the ceremonial meal or later, with non-leading questions, and they all reported similar phenomena. They also told me E.R. had the same opinion, as would the other sweaters. As a newcomer I was too self-conscious to ask the Indians or E.R. I feared my skepticism or wonder would be perceived as a lack of belief, something I was not willing to do, and had no inclination.

I know what I believed I experienced and believe others experienced but offer little in way of explanation. During the third round at the height of the intensity of the singing, I noticed a sound discernible from the singing. It began as a hum and at its peak was a low pitched roar. The earth felt to be vibrating much as it would in other circumstances that came to mind. My first thought was that it was a mild earthquake, my second that it might be a fully loaded tractor trailer truck, pulling out with a lot of torque nearby, and I thought maybe it was a train going by on a nearby track I was unaware of, or a low flying plane or helicopter. I could not figure out what made the noise and vibrating earth. I had mentally gone through the possibilities one by one, so I know it lasted more than five seconds, but probably less than twenty-five, probably the phenomena was observable for around fifteen to twenty seconds. After the singing and the round was over E.R. thanked Grandfather Buffalo for his appearance and thanked him for the healing he brought. Afterward I asked Eve and Edie and two other Anglos and they all told me Grandfather Buffalo had come with great power to bring his healing. They seemed to treat the event as something that indicated a very powerful sweat and that it meant good things for all who took part. I have experienced three earthquakes in California, and do not believe that such a mild vibration of the earth would have produced the sound that accompanied the vibrations. Gunter's son Chris had been the doorman directly outside of the sweat, less than fifteen feet away, and I asked him if he had noticed anything. He related what a quiet peaceful night it had been. So I asked him if any large trucks had gone down that reservation dirt road, and he said no. So I asked if there were train tracks nearby, and he said no, so I asked about low flying planes, helicopters, anything that could disturb a quiet desert night, and he said no that it had been a quiet and peaceful, uneventful night. I was aware enough of hypnosis and the phenomena associated with altered states to not be surprised that those that believed and carried strong expectations could experience such an event, which is not out of context with folk-lore. I carried no such expectation, and did not receive any suggestion singling out Grandfather Buffalo, which is why I was surprised to experience something I did not expect, or even believe possible. The thing that perplexed me most was why I perceived something I did not expect or desire, while Chris, standing so nearby experienced nothing.

The only explanation I was to receive was that the noise and vibration was that of a herd of buffalo, not physical buffalo, but those of spirit sent by Grandfather Buffalo. Eve later told me a story about one of her relatives in the Canadian military of the past, who experienced a sweat lodge where Grandfather deer or antelope or some such hoofed creature was invoked. When he came out of the sweat there were hoof prints all over the igloo-shaped sweat lodge.

Those last two rounds E.R. worked on me, but he was not actively working on me during the described phenomena. He did some of the things he did before and again the eagle fans felt incredibly hot. I have an uncertain memory of E.R. sucking on my head and throwing up, although this is a vague memory and I have no exact records of the date or round he did it. I know that it made me feel uncomfortable to think that something bad or evil in me needed to come out and would make a shaman sick when he took it from me and then got rid of it. I can remember him sucking on my head, going towards the rocks, and retching.

When the third round was over I could notice the buzzing and surging energy in my body I described in earlier sweats. E.R. lay towards the open flap and bodies laid about everywhere. E.R. would have this very far-away look in his eyes after the second and third rounds, and I often would wonder if he was going to bring himself back to conduct the ritual, which he unfailingly did. E.R. had impressed me with the dignity, the humility, and the beauty of his ritual work.

He was a huge, strong man, who conducted his ceremonies with great humility before the Great Spirit, serving as both an example and inspiration. His movements were sure and his rituals precise, he let people know what was happening, and what to do. Sometimes before the next round would start, after people had sat up and regrouped their energies, he would sometimes give moral advice.

E.R. might give moral advice in general or to a specific person. He might just mention something and elongate on it later in private after the ceremonial meal. During a regular Sunday sweat he might answer questions put to him beforehand in private. During my last sweat he warned me again that temptation would come my way; that the things I had done were good, and I had to maintain that good state of mind. He mentioned then and expounded on later that I should wear socks all the time: that my feet stayed too cold, that I should eat more in general, and eat more meat and fish, and it would be best if I could hunt and fish for some of this. He told me to really watch my temper. He told me to pray hard and to pray to the grandfather animal spirit and to work with my animal spirit; and now that I had sweated four days, I had to rest four days.

Before the fourth round started I took the opportunity to state my thanks and appreciation. I started thanking the Great Spirit, the Earth Mother, all the healing spirits who had helped, then I thanked E.R. for the sweat lodge, and his work, and I thanked all who had sweated. Such verbal expressions are not mandatory, but probably are the norm. But I noticed then and later that the individual was accepted as they were, and some people not given to talk or public expression rarely if ever spoke during sweat. People would ask permission to, and express what they felt moved to express: I never observed or felt any social pressure exerted to illicit or inhibit such verbal expression.

During the fourth round I felt both exhilarated and exhausted. My feet and hands continued to buzz and tingle, and the thank-you songs were enthusiastic. From the length of the rounds and the way everybody was sprawled out at the end of the rounds, and the time it took to regain composure and sit up, the others shared my exhaustion

Finally E.R. said to bless ourselves and people reached with their bare hands or with their sage toward the steam and then patted their heads and bodies. The last water hissed on the rocks and the sound of metal against rock could be heard as E.R. placed the empty bucket upside down upon the rocks, as the final and enthusiastic Ho!s were shouted out. When the front and back flaps were finally opened and that blessed cool air poured in, the bodies, mine included could have been corpses for all the apparent movement. Most of us there had been through two or three hours a day, for four days straight, of the most arduous exposure to heat, steam, unnaturally rapid and intense sweating and dehydration. We were slower that day than we had been previously to sit up and clean-up and receive the pipe.

While I waited for the sacred pipe I was leaning back against the wall of the sweat lodge side with my eyes closed. The thought came to me very strongly that I would be leaving this sacred environment and returning to the secular world, so I felt strongly moved to make a pact with myself that for a minimum of two months I would follow Eve's suggestions of total abstinence from alcohol, pot, etc. Because of the time and place and inspiration I considered this a sacred pact with myself and I did, in fact keep it.

When the sacred pipe came to me I smoked it aware that I was more comfortable praying and smoking with E.R.'s pipe than I had been initially. I fought off my exhaustion while smoking, because as I smoked I went through my prayers of thanks, thanking all the Powers and spirits, giving thanks for the gift of an animal spirit, and praying for all who had sweated and helped with the sweat, I thanked for healing, prayed for continued healing, and as always, prayed for the healing of the Earth Mother. When I handed E R. the pipe I became aware of the exhaustion returning.

My hands and feet were buzzing and I felt shaky when I crawled out behind E.R. Chris had already brought my chair around and with my final effort I transferred up into it. At that point I sort of fainted, but I don't believe that I fully lost consciousness, I simply didn't have the physical strength to sit up, or perform any other voluntary movement.

I remained motionless and unaware as the others came out until I felt strong, but feminine hands, one on each shoulder, pulling me back and up into a sitting position from behind. Then I felt a hand on either side of my face, and opened my eyes to find Eve standing in front of me. I closed my eyes again and breathed deeply. Edie was behind me, Eve was in front and I was aware that they were breathing deeply and regularly, and I figured out that they were transferring to me, willing into my body, some of their Life-force. This continued for maybe a minute or two, and besides physically reviving I experienced the subjective feelings of joy and love from and for these two who had made possible and then shared this healing, which is so beneficial and simultaneously torturous.

I could sit up on my own and had regained my composure when Eve kissed my forehead and she and Edie moved to go inside. At that point a wind blew and I felt the wind lift the hair on my right leg. I immediately told them and then hollered to E.R. and told him.

His comment was that I would feel even more that it was just the beginning. The others went to change while I experimented trying to discover any other noticeable difference of sensation or function, but could find none. Still the sensation of the wind had been strong and spontaneous, and I took it as a good sign, even if I couldn't replicate or improve the sensation.

The ceremonial meals went as before, and this final one seemed especially warm and joyous. Although it was not the same people exactly, every day, it was the same core, and the shared suffering and experience had created strong bonds between us. How could I not feel close to people like Paul and Lilly, who had nothing to gain, and had never met me before, and had no code or responsibility to compel them, yet had prayed and suffered for my healing. During the meal and conversation afterward many people talked to me, both openly and privately, relevant to the sweats. Donna had experienced a dream in which I rose from my wheelchair and took two steps, falling towards the north. Others contributed their hopes and positive feelings. E.R. reiterated the things he mentioned earlier about wearing socks, eating fish and meat, not getting angry, and the certainty that the other side would come at me. He also told me to try to stand and walk, to try every day.

He told me to pray to the Grandfather and work with my animal spirit, using food or tobacco. He said it was all up to the Big Man and if I wanted it bad enough, and worked for it I could have it.

Maria, who had from the first always done everything she possibly could to make me feel comfortable and cared for, talked to me privately after the meal. She said that while we had been inside the sweat lodge that she had felt Christ touch me. She said this with a sincerity and conviction that left my body was immediately covered in "goose bumps."

Through conversation with Eve and E.R. a kind of strategy immerged for my immediate future. While I remained in California would continue to visit Eve when convenient. I could not remain full time, she had speaking engagements and travel plans and others must pass through and take my place to learn or be healed. But when convenient, I would continue with her as before and come to the regular Sunday sweats, I would visit E.R. every so often.

They would take a wait and see attitude about my healing progress, before deciding whether another four day sweat needed.

Warriors of the Rainbow

The next four days were days of rest, recovery, and assimilation I spent my time eating, drinking water, resting, writing, and praying. Once a day I would join Eve, and sometimes Edie, as she smoked the sacred pipe on the nearby mountain. As I read back in my journal my comments return to the theme of love.

"All the people Eve has introduced me to have incredible love, incredible love. I`m learning very, very much, although not learning so much specific techniques, though some - but mostly love."

These comments out of context would make one think that the author must be some honey-dripping Pollyannaish. But these comments must be considered in relation to the fact that most of these people were met and related to before, during, and after, sacred ritual. By analogy I knew that if I met someone only at church my knowledge of their behavior and complexity was limited compared to that of someone whom I met in various secular activities. I'm sure these people were no different; I knew I was meeting the religiously active, at their place of religious practice, within a religious context.

One ethnographic observation not yet discussed was the prevalent use of tobacco, in a secular context, by many of the sweaters, before and after sweat, and also in their daily life. Cigarette smoking was widespread, especially hand rolled Bull Durham or Prince Albert. I pondered why a health conscious group would contain so many smokers, and wandered if it was because Indians had always had tobacco, that was used both in sacred and secular context, or if these people smoked because it was one of the few secular pleasures they didn't deny themselves.

Eve was pleased with my progress and continued to stress offering oneself as an open channel to the healing white light, and utilizing the intuition to follow divine Will. She said we'd all been given a Divine spark, but we could offer ourselves back as a flame. I had become aware of some of the differences between Eve and E.R. and decided that Eve stressed both the mental framework and the experience, while E.R. considered the process not mental but simply opening up to the experience of reality and following the heart.

There had appeared to be acknowledgment of sexual roles and differentiation at the sweat, and within the Paiute families I had meet. Judging on three examples the sexual roles and differentiation remains stronger in Paiute culture than in mainstream culture where they have been eroded. Although Paiute Women have always been shaman there was a traditional sexual differentiation in relation to the sweats. Before assimilation the men had big communal sweats, while the women were restricted to a small style sweat lodge. not unlike E.R.'s. Now both sexes sweated together in the small plains style sweat, but I personally have never seen a woman tend the fire, carry rocks, or run a sweat. I have seen women be the doorman, after men carried the rocks in, a woman may lift and close the flaps between rounds. I have never seen a woman run a sweat, although years later on another reservation, I knew of a woman who owned a sweat lodge, had one on her property and the hosted the ceremonial meals inside her horns, but she attended sweats there, run by men, and she never conducted them herself.

Eve made it clear to me that she was aware of the cultural differences and had to respect them, but she thought their breakdown was in the future and she hoped it came quick. Eve believed in the equality of the sexes.

During the four days of the sweat I had felt a change in the way E.R. related to me. When I had first come to visit Eve I had been introduced as her student and a healer and all the Anglos seemed to take this seriously. E.R. and Maria had seemed to concentrate on my role as a patient and never made much reference to my studies and work under Eve's direction. I was aware that my ego desired that same respect from the Paiute shaman and his wife, but they continued to concentrate on my role as patient in need of healing.

In all fairness Maria wasn't dealing with that aspect of things, I only received from her, kindness and prayers, and a serious desire for my healing. At first I felt E.R. considered me a responsibility he had assumed long ago as a healer, that even if a white man or woman, girl or boy shows up, and asks respectfully and properly – a healing is granted. I knew respect isn't something other people acquire for you with a recitation of your good deeds, rather it is something an individual must earn.

I was aware that the respect and affection I desired to receive from the shaman could only be earned in time, so I concentrated on fulfilling my role in the sweats. t knew from what E.R. and Eve said that since I had come to the Indians for healing it was very important that I show respect for the "Indian Way" and I tried hard to do this, by learning to perform ritual correctly and following Paiute etiquette. There was a noticeable difference in the way E.R. treated me as the four days progressed. Some of this could easily be written off as just becoming more comfortable around a previous stranger because of shared experiences, but that is not what I mean. As the four days progressed I attempted to follow his directions and put my heart into it. But two specific events seemed to be landmark changes in the way he perceived me.

The first of these was when his animal spirit brought an animal spirit for me. This is an indication of the spontaneous freedom of the shaman while working, although he invokes the spirits and rules the sweat lodge, his visions and perceptions do not follow his expectations, he reports what he sees. His surprise at my being provided a spirit seemed so genuine I could not doubt it.

The second event that brought about a change was his perception that during one of the last sweats, more spirits became manifest in one round than he had ever experienced in his sweat lodge. As the four days progressed, especially the last two, I felt that E.R. treated me much more warmly, and even would joke and kid with me sometimes. The change was not drastic but discernible and I felt much better for it.

Over the next two months when I would come to visit Eve and go to sweat, sometimes, usually in the middle of the week, Eve would arrange for me to go and visit E.R. I had initially thought that these visits would be like my sessions with Eve, but I was wrong. I went expecting to find out about E.R.'s metaphysical outlook and more detailed information about how and why he did what he did.

At first these sessions seemed disappointing because no such revelations were forthcoming. I thought at first this may be due to language barriers, or racial distrust, but years later I talked to a young Indian who enlightened me. He said that E.R. was not known as a teacher, but that people came to him because he performed his rituals so beautifully and powerfully. He told me that E.R. taught by example, by the humility with which he performed his ritual and lived his life. This made me feel better about the whole process, because my questions all seemed to have been answered in the same way. I would ask E.R. something, maybe complex, yet the answer came back as simplicity. I was real, the Heavenly Father is real, I didn`t need to think my way there, but open up in heart, and just experience the reality. If I asked him about specifics, as in relation to my animal spirit, he would tell me what he did, or what was traditional, but that I must do what feels right and what I was lead to do by the Grandfathers.

I finally told him about my vision of a pipe and asked him if he thought I could have a pipe. He told me that once I was well we could talk about it. When I described the pipe for him, he told me that even if I got well he could not carve the pipe for it was a different style and tradition than the ones he carved. This left me puzzled because I thought I was supposed to be true to the vision, so the pipe issue got pushed back to a back burner, and left as a concern for the future.

I don`t know what motivated me but when I thought I had gained a certain amount of acceptance I asked E.R., "what about Wovoka?". He looked me straight in the eye and said he`d never heard of him. Needless to say the subject did not come back up in later conversations.

During the next two months I would come and go, and as part of my training visit people Eve sent me to that were in her craft network. She offered letters of introduction to two well-known medicine men, gut they were at too great a distance. One of the most important of these was called Dr. Gail Pierce, a highly respected nurse, was an unconventional healer, a Buddhist who personally knew the Dali Llama. Reportedly he had spent the night once at her house in San Jose. I was also sent to a chiropractor, among others. I would also visit friends I made in the Fresno area.

Whenever I visited with Eve the previous pattern of prayer and smoking the Sacred Pipe was resumed. Eve had speaking engagements and many visitors, so sometimes I camped out on the mountain or stayed in a hotel if a room at Edie's was not available.

My journal records, "Eve is raising me, preparing me to be a more effective soldier in the Army of light. She is a veteran of so many conflicts it is scary, but to those who dwell in their Creator all things are possible." The day came, rather unexpectedly, when Eve and I went up on the mountain like normal, but this time she challenged me.

Up until this point we had much discussion concerning the war between the Army of Darkness and the Army of Light. I had questioned the use of the term darkness, being a lover of the night and moonlight.

She assured me that the usage was symbolic, that the day and night were equally holy and that the word darkness was used in lieu of terms such as evil, death, or dissolution. She faced me and recounted: that she had accepted me as her student, taught me, answered my questions, smoked with me, healed me, and introduced me into the sweat lodge. She said she had taught me as much as she could up to a point, but that it was TIME FOR COMMITMENT.

She said the strength of my personal will and my desire for personal power made me easier prey and more likely to be seduced by the Army of Darkness. She said if that was my choice: that they would certainly show up to accept me. But if I wanted to continue on with her I was going to have to join the Army of Light.

She said if I wanted to hang on to my supposed neutrality I could suffer under that illusion, but that the sweats I was clean and shining and being actively recruited, and that a choice was unavoidable with the passage of time

The challenge was clear as were the options that went with it, I could embrace evil and pay the price, or I could go on without her and try to stay neutral, or I could continue on with her, having accepted my role and responsibility as an active warrior in that war for the Army of Light. So up on one of the highest mountains of this continent, I made my commitment and was sworn in as a member of a spiritual army in a constant and unrelenting state of war. I became a Spiritual Warrior of the Rainbow. I took a sacred oath to heal the sick and to fight evil. The rainbow links heaven and Earth, and the colors represent the unity of all races, of all the created. I have seen this term in print in the books of the Medicine man Sun Bear, and I heard Eve use it publicly, so I assumed that this was not Q-B-L and or a big secret. Whether there is any actual earthly official organization using this term is doubtful, but possible. Later research revealed that many tribes currently tell of prophesies of a time when the world will be sick and dying and the spiritual warriors of the rainbow would rise to save it. From the Cree to the Eskimos to Hopi to the Sioux, many tribes have prophesies concerning Indians who have kept alive the rituals and old ways. Some tribes' prophesies say these will join with like-thinking whites and theses spiritual warriors of the rainbow will lead the way back to reverence of Nature and save the planet. The 1962 book *Warriors of the Rainbow* by William Willoya and Vinson Brown was said they have influenced the early environmentalist who went on to found Greenpeace.

My specific instructions concerning this new responsibility was to attempt to heal those that asked for healing, and continue to strive to fulfill Divine Will, and to fight and cast out what Eve called the demons and beasties of the Army of Darkness. I found the word beastie as humorous, but she used it to denote a sub-demon, a lesser spirit of evil. I was instructed to constantly cleanse my energy field, to bring the white-light down to fill and flow through my aura, and to use the protective circle of White light, and in my imagination to regularly put on the complete armor of Cod. This comes from Ephesians in the bible, and in the entire book is the only prescribed protection against the demonic forces. Eve echoed E.R.'s warning saying that the temptations would become even stronger after making such a commitment. I was warned against the future use of drugs, and alcohol. She told me to never, never get drunk, especially to the point of passing out, because that would leave me wide open to demonic attack and at least temporary possession. I was not to really have much understanding of all this until months later when I assisted Eve in reversing a case of psychic attack, and in an exorcism. These events were in eclectic, non-Indian circumstances, in San Jose, and there was no doubt in my mind that those involved took both psychic attach and possession as serious realities. I was told to protect myself every night and every morning; that the conflict was constant.

I had found from conversation that both the wolf and the coyote were prominent animals in Paiute Myth, with wolf as more of a culture hero and coyote as a trickster spirit. But coyote was not purely evil, he represented good things as well, he was more the Great Spirit`s instrument of temptation. In the sweat lodge the forces of evil, disease, death and injury were treated in a general way, they were never described, or treated as entities or animal spirits.

I had considered the dreams that were unpleasant and unwanted circumstances of daily life, to be the method and form of the pre-warned about temptations and attacks. I did have an experience, although, that brought my understanding more in line with Eve and E.R.`s warnings.

One night I had returned on a Saturday night, planning to attend the Sunday sweat. Eve probably had some other guests, I was camping out on the mountain and the fall night had grown chilly. MY fire burned out, the night was cold, and I was very tired from the day's driving. I decided instead of sitting up in the cold air and going through my nightly prayers and protection, I would stay inside my sleeping bag and say a much abbreviated version.

I did so sleepily and drifted off to sleep. Eve had taught me that there were two kinds of dreams; those of your normal psychological function, and those of a deeper spiritual meaning, which are much more vivid and meaningful.

My experience that night was of the second variety, but at the time I did not believe I was dreaming. I was asleep when I thought I was awakened by the presence of animals. Two coyotes approached me from the right. I lay in the sleeping bag hoping they would ignore me. Instead they walked up, sniffed at the bag, and grabbed me with their teeth. They weren't trying to bite through, but I could feel the pressure of their teeth, and it was not gentle. I felt the firm pressure and pain of sharp teeth on my right arm and right leg. My immediate response was to growl like an animal in an attempt to drive them away. The teeth closed harder. It came to me to use the clockwise circle of white light. In my imagination I began drawing the circle of white in the north and by the time the light was a quarter of the circle in the east, the coyotes vanished. I completed the circle of white light and began to pray for protection.

I did this for a while and then drifted back to sleep, and in the following dream My two older brothers appeared, and I was comforted and felt protected by their presence. I awoke later, before the sun had risen, with a clear image of both dreams, although the second was much less clear and vivid than the first.

I knew that sunrise was not that much longer and that future rest and sleep were unlikely, I was too spooked by what had happened. So I got my stuff together and loaded my car, figuring I would drive down into town and hope the restaurant opened early. That was my plan, but my car wouldn't start. I didn't want to kill the battery, so I would try and then wait, try and wait. I did this for forty-five minutes as the sun began to rise. When the sun finally rose fully over the mountains in the east, and the day had come, sunlight hit the hood of my car and my car started. I flew down that mountain.

I told Eve before sweat what had happened and she reiterated her instructions for morning and nighttime prayers. After the sweat, I told E.R. about my experience and he looked at me with a look that made me imagine and hear his thoughts" well what did you expect, you dumb shit, you think we're making all this up?" I don't know if his thoughts were as crude as mine, but I'm sure I got the right message.

My attendance of the Sunday sweats was good for me in many ways. I got to go to sweats that weren't centered on me, and so I became a participant like everybody else. I got to meet many more

Paiutes and also Indians from other tribes. I was able to watch the interaction between Anglos and Indians, both as strangers and old friends. I also got to meet other medicine men who were traveling and they would come to sweat with E.R.

My most memorable instance of sweating with another medicine man was when Rainbow Dick helped E.R. run his Sunday Sweat. Rainbow Dick was a medicine man who made his living making jewelry and then travelling around selling it.

Rainbow Dick was called that because during his travels he had spread his method of trying to heal the earth. The sweat was no different than other sweats, except that during the third round E.R. would turn it over to Dick to lead his healing. Dick began by saying that every person had all the colors within their soul and that when they poured from the heart each individual had his own rainbow, his unique combinations of colors. Then Dick lead a healing in which everybody would direct the rainbow colors of their soul to pour out from their heart and join together in a circle over the rocks. Once everybody had sent out and joined their colors in the center, Dick would direct the joint rainbows of our souls down into the Earth to heal and replenish the Earth our Mother who provides us with all things. Dick had said the earth provides for us, but all we do is take, take, take, and pollute, pollute, pollute, and that this was a way to give back love and healing.

Many of us found this a profound and moving experience. I was also glad to be learning more about how these people had been raised and what their lives today were like. I noticed early on that the Native American men most likely to speak with Anglo strangers had military tattoos. Many would inquire if my disability was service related. The other Indians I met who would be likely to exhibit little social distance were those who had gone to college, or traveled widely, or worked in large cities in the Anglo world. There was little social distance seemingly between Indian strangers, and a difference of tribe did not seem to matter. Indeed I learned that Indians from many different tribes would be sent away to the same boarding school, and that there was much inter-tribal dating and marriage. I met also mixed couples and all three were Indian men married to Anglo women. There was definite social distance between some Paiutes and Anglos unknown to each other. Although this was always reduced by the sweat, it was not always overcome. I would attempt to observe social distance by watching people and the degree to which they interacted, how relaxed and spontaneous it was, and whether their body language revealed anxiety or natural calmness.

I have mentioned that Paiute attendance was often a family affair but I don`t know what base number of families might look immediately to E.R. for spiritual help when needed, or attend regularly for spiritual nourishment. Eve told me that E.R. desired more of his people from the Christian and non-religious ranks to get involved with his sweat lodge, just as he longed for the missing young men. Eve had told me of stirrings of racial trouble, but I did not witness any that first trip. I returned to Georgia for Christmas deeply impressed with what a harmonious situation I had experienced at E.R.'s sweat lodge.

At this point having revealed the thoughts and workings of an Anglo shaman and the Sweat lodge ritual of a Paiute shaman, I must address the three questions of social and ideological conflict.

1) **Will the ancient and secret traditions and practices remain secret and closed, or will they become more open, will they be shared with non-Indians?**

Information teaching the basics of the native outlook on Nature and the Great Spirit as well as outlines of rituals like the sweat lodge and Sun Dance has been around and on the increase since the 1930's. E.R. knew this. I have described the process by which his sweat lodge became integrated. E.R. himself did not teach as much as provide the opportunity to experience certain realties. If you took the opportunity and had the experience, he might answer your questions about it. Indians and Anglos both were secretive about sweat attendance to other Anglos, and knew that some sacred subjects were to be discussed only at the proper time and place. E.R.'s sweat was selectively integrated, he had to meet you and approve before you could attend, and you had to agree not to reveal names or locations. The relationships of the participants seemed to be warm, and E.R. seemed to spend a lot of time with Bill, and Cunter was learning to be a singer of the sacred songs. At this time E.R.'s tradition and practices was selectively open and selectively shared.

What effect will Jesus and Christianity have on traditional belief and practice?

It would have been hard to distinguish what the difference would be between the Paiute Heavenly Father and the Christian. E.R. often referred to God as a Father. He did call on Jesus in prayer and would instruct the sweaters that it was O.K. to pray to Jesus. There seemed no conflict between the two, but Jesus was only prayed to and not actively worked with. In fact the large majority of sweaters were Christian. Some of the local ministers, however, would refer to the sweat as a work of the devil, but this was not unanimous among the clergy .Jesus was most often mentioned in the first and fourth rounds when the generalized invocations and thank-yous were said, and not real often past that, during the sweats.

3) **Will the impersonal and mechanical view of Nature promulgated by the dominant culture have an effect on traditional belief and practice?**

To the extent that the shaman today is exclusively a spiritual healer and leaves the physical side to the M.D.'s is a lasting change. I have been in sweat when a child outside was cut, and the sweat was barely interrupted as an older relative outside was instructed to take the child to the emergency room at the nearest hospital..

There is little influence of the scientific-mechanical world inside the sweat lodge. The sweat seems to reaffirm the traditional outlook on Nature for the Paiutes and influence the Anglo to adopt that outlook. The Paiute shaman is a Master of Spirits in 1985, as was his predecessors 30,000 to 100,000 years ago.

The First Schism

While I was in Georgia what I will refer to as the first schism occurred. My sources of information at the time were letters and phone conversations with Eve and Edie. My sources afterward were what the different Anglos told me upon my return, and still later, in Eve's book *I Send a Voice*. What I heard then and tell now is basically the way the Anglos perceived what happened.

Eve had talked about and showed concern about increasing political and racial tension in the valley. Bill and Gunter were so firmly established as fixtures of E.R.'s sweat, always there if needed, that at first I hoped Eve was exaggerating the swift decline of racial harmony within the valley as a whole and the sweat lodge specifically.

Things continued to degenerate until the absolute low point was reached and E.R. demanded Eve's pipe back, and expelled all the Anglos from his sweat lodge.

The social forces that brought this schism about are complex and if understanding is to be achieved the differences between the generalized outlooks of Eve and E.R.'s different craft networks must be explored in relation to long term attendance and participation patterns of E.R.'s sweat lodge.

The relationship between E.R. and Eve, along with some mutually shared medicine men friends, was the point of intersection between two different craft networks. I use the term craft network to denote a loose and unofficial group of people who consider themselves as peers, or at least engaged in similar activities. From the individuals perspective it would be those people he would participate in ritual with, or work with, or feel shared common beliefs and practices with, and mutual respect.

Eve had a more eclectic craft network that E.R. Eve as an author, speaker, and teacher was known in some circles on a national level. E.R.

on the other hand, had shunned any kind of public exposure.

Eve's network included people of various faiths and persuasions, and healers who practiced widely differing crafts. Though she and E.R. had mutual friends that were medicine men and women, they also had such associations not shared with the other.

Medicine men such as Heymyost Storm and Sun Bear had very similar outlooks and the books and lives of these three represent a certain movement on the American social scene. All three had the perception that the beauty and truth of the Indian way was desperately needed in America and beyond. They saw the massive spiritual dissatisfaction of modern man and the wholesale destruction and pollution of Nature as problems that could be greatly remedied if enough people would accept the Indian Way of respect for Nature and the direct experience of spiritual realities.

Sunbear is a great believer in the Rainbow and he began what is known as the Bear Tribe and opened it to all people who would respect and live the Indian Way. He is a Chippewa Medicine man who started the Bear tribe to let it be an instrument for the dissemination of the sacred pipe, the sweat, and treating the Mother Earth as sacred - to whomever would respectfully live the life. He writes, travels, speaks, and helps direct the self-owned communities.

Heymyost Storm is a Cheyenne Medicine man of Cheyenne and Scandinavian descent. He wrote the classic *Seven Arrows*. He also began the North American Metis Association. This was a group with a function much like the Bear Tribe, to give those that had the desire to accept the Indian way a sense of belonging and a vehicle to share knowledge. The term metis is French meaning mixed. Its` original meaning meant one of mixed Indian-Anglo blood, but Storm reasoned that in melting pot America, anyone who isn`t pure whatever can consider themselves metis.

Sun Bear and Hyemeyohsts Storm and others like them are

sometimes referred to as media-medicine men. It is true that they do write, speak, and travel, convinced the world will be a better place as more people adopt what they consider to be the traditional outlook. When this term of media medicine men is used derogatorily, it is often by what can be called the reservation-medicine men. To these men their secret traditions should remain such and although they might widely travel among reservations they are squarely against disseminating the pipe or the sweat to non-Indians. They do not feel it is appropriate for medicine men to publicly discuss their sacred traditions or display the sacred pipe.

At that time and to my knowledge E.R. did not have any of the media-medicine people in his Craft network, other than Eve. From what I understand his network included people with a diversity of attitudes towards race and secrecy. On one extreme there are medicine men who don`t sweat with whites, are blatantly racist, and openly anti-white. On the other extreme were medicine men that were themselves of some mixed ancestry, or else had relatives in mixed marriages and were not going to exclude anyone purely because of race. In the middle are some who think the world benefitted from the dissemination of some Indian lore and the philosophy of the Indian way, they did not think medicine people should make public displays of themselves or reveal specifics.

Despite the diversity of opinions of his fellow medicine men E.R.'s sweat had existed and worked harmoniously on a selectively integrated basis for almost a decade. When he had decided to go past being a pipe-maker and become a shaman in the mid-sixties he opened his sweat lodge where he lived, in an area that had not had one for some time. E.R. reportedly did not receive the widespread support and participation he had hoped for. The local population was divided between:

- those who were totally assimilated and did not cherish their traditions but had adopted the dominant culture's materialism

- those that drank and partied and were not actively religious

- those that cherished their traditions but were not spiritually active

- those that were traditional and spiritually active

- Christians who would come to sweat

- Christians who thought it devilish, and would not.

E.R. probably found out that there were not as many traditionally minded people willing to be active as he had thought, and that the distances involved and the transportation requirements kept the attendance and participation below the level he had expected.

From almost the very start of his sweat lodge, Eve attended, and gradually came the others. E.R. had worked with Bill and brought them in himself. Sweats are held for various reasons; the weekly Sunday sweat, a single or four day healing sweat, a thanks-giving sweat for something good, sweats before and after the two, three, and four night fasts of the rising Pipe-Healer, or before and after any fast for guidance or spiritual nourishment. Once an Anglo was accepted into his sweat as a regular member it seems he or she was as eligible to fast and sweat as any Paiute. Of the nine Anglos I knew, two men and two women had received a personal or family pipe. To my knowledge only Edie was preparing for the pipe-healer fasts; and I have mentioned that Gunter was learning to be a singer. Sometimes Gunter would accompany E.R. on his trips to establish new sweats. I have said that at any sweat three to six of the Anglos might show up. Attendance at a sweat varies greatly, rarely a sweat would have as few as six to eight participants, the average was between nine to sixteen, and a large sweat would be seventeen to the low twenties. At eighteen the sweat is full but comfortable, much past that is very crowded. These numbers indicate the extent to which E.R.'s sweat lodge had become integrated. Although it might have been unusual, it was possible for a Paiute to show up at sweat and find the Indians outnumbered by the Anglos. This degree of integration and training of Anglos was something that E.R. came under attack for in the events which precipitated the expulsion of the Anglos.

It was not unusual for E.R. to disappear for days or weeks at a time. He said sometimes he would wander in the wilderness alone, but there were assumptions that medicine men would gather in secret and perform ritual, maybe of a higher degree or greater complexity than that shared with the uninitiated. His disappearances were a reality, the rest was speculation. It was after such a disappearance that E.R. came back with a different attitude towards the Anglos, and a different way of doctoring.

The events that preceded this happened over a relatively short period of time compared to ten years of harmony. The national political picture was a time of intense political activity including within a few years you had the Wounded Knee uprising, the Peltier sham trial and conviction, and the Longest Walk, which carried a sacred pipe across the U.S. and encircled the F.B.I. building with it (which I attended), and finally the passing of The American Indian Freedom of Religion Act of 1977. There were many groups like the militant American Indian Movement championing the cause of native pride and identity. Detractors often accused some of these people for talking their spiritual tradition but not living it, preferring the macho drinking, fighting - warrior lifestyle of the radical political activist. It was a time of political action and activity, and there were activist traveling, beating the bushes and drumming up support.

Political activist from the outside came into the valley and sought out the politically active of the valley. There are some activist without hate or racial prejudice, and some who are resentful racist.

The activist who came into the valley in found out about E.R.`s sweat and didn`t like it. Their reasoning was possibly that they wanted to prevent Anglos from "stealing their tradition" as I heard one say years later, or that of protection. The protection scenario runs... the white man couldn't live harmoniously where he was, having no peace with himself, Nature, or God so he came over here to steal the land from the Indians. Because he is ruthless and has no respect for nature he develops machines and weapons of death and destruction superior to the peoples of nature which he conquers. To absolve his guilt he takes his rifle and makes you pick up a Bible. Because he is Godless and power hungry he corrupts all things. His religion no longer satisfies him so now he wants ours; just watch how the power-mad corrupters come into our religion to control and corrupt it too, And this will happen if we don't stop it right now.

Needless to say they were less than thrilled about Gunther, and the four Anglos with pipes. The fact that Eve was speaking publicly about her work as a Pipe Healer seemed to enrage them and they said that E.R.

was responsible for Eve and that she was misusing a Pipe and talking about things she shouldn`t. And then there was also the irritation of her book.

I don`t know if the social forces directed at E.R. were part of a planned intentional campaign or not, the Anglos thought so.

The radical activist from the outside joined by those of the valley began to make E.R.`s sweat a focus of public opinion within the community of Indians. They received support from the racist reservation-medicine men in the area that had never approved anyway, and solicited support from others like them in nearby areas. Pressure was put directly on E.R. and the Paiutes who attended the sweats to oust the Anglos and restrain Eve. Some of the Paiutes swept up in the revitalization movement who were new to the sweat lodge and had just had begun attending in the last year were for it, and the Anglos felt their old friends from many years at the sweat lodge did not stand up to this pressure vocally or adamantly enough.

The Anglos were dismayed when friends that had previously shared their lives left them alone, silence and suspicion replaced conversation and friendship. Indians who had never gone to a sweat and never would had strong opinion and things grew more polarized. Of course those uninvolved but of a resentful and racist disposition joined right in.

The activist came to E.R. and explained that one reason the youth had not come and more Indians hadn`t participated was the presence of the Anglos. They assured him that the number of his people involved would grow by expelling the whites, and that his statue and influence as a leader of his people would grow.

The local and outside activists, the regional and outside racist reservation medicine men, a few of the sweaters, and the local Indian racists all put pressure on E.R. and the Paiute sweaters. The Anglos sat watching a one way battle, helpless and feeling abandoned by their friends who they thought should do more, should fight harder.

Eve was in the East taking care of speaking engagements and healing requests, when E.R. disappeared. I don't know any Anglo that saw him leave, and am pretty positive no Anglos went with him, but there were theories about what had happened.

The most prevalent composite theory is that E.R. went off with some of the medicine men in his craft network, and some from outside of our area. These were of the secret, closed, reservation medicine men anti-white persuasion. They saw the white man as the enemy of nature and the enemy of Indian. They strongly disapproved of integrated sweats and of Eve's publicity. There was a strong and persistent rumor about a black South African witch doctor. I have heard E.R. talk about this man but don't know that he was at the rituals where E.R. was converted to accepting their viewpoint.

A virulent Indian and a virulent witch doctor would be a strong combination of anti-white philosophy. The most exotic of the theories said that it was simple black magic, negative psychic energy, amplified through ritual, hidden behind terms of saving and preserving the traditions.

While he was thusly being indoctrinated he was also learning a new way to doctor that was not of local origin. To help the reader understand it must be explained that some of the most traditional and well versed, full medicine men in the old sense of the term, as a master of positive and negative forces, were of this closed, secret persuasion. Some of these will also be adamantly anti-Christian, but that was not the emphasis of this conflict. It was put to him by traditionals he respected that he needed to stand up as a leader of his people, he needed to expel the whites from the sweat lodge, and he needed to correct Eve.

When E.R. returned he assembled the Anglos and informed them:

- that his sweat was going to be for Indians only now

- it was what his people wanted and needed. However, because he had taken the same healing oath Eve had, swearing to heal all the sick who asked, regardless,

- they could come occasionally as visitors, or if they were really sick.

- He told those that had pipes not to misuse them, and

- he dismissed them, asking them to pray for him.

Needless to say the Anglos were shocked and hurt, especially the two men, Bill and Gunter, who had considered him as a father or best friend. They felt abandoned by their spiritual father and by other friends of many years.

Eve returned without knowledge of these events and went immediately to visit E.R. and report on her trip. She came in and he yelled at her, screaming that she had misused her pipe, used it selfishly and showed off with it. He demanded that she give him her pipe. She had never seen him like this and was scared of the intensity of his anger; he was a large, strong powerful man. He was huge, furious, and hostile. There were angry exchanges, she denied his right to take her pipe, and it was given to her under the direction of their mutual teacher – Grandfather Harris, although E.R. had carved it. After more exchanges she swore solemnly that she had not and would not misuse her pipe. Less angrily than before he asked her again to go get her pipe and she did.

He took the pipe from her and rubbed it with sage and then censed it with sweet grass. He was breaking his bond with her, dissolving his responsibility for her and her pipe, setting her free. He told her to go take care of the people, and he meant the Anglos, the white people. The disciplining of Eve and the expelling of the Anglos seemed to placate the activist need for change, satisfied them, and proved their influence and that of the local activists/traditionals. At that point the subject of the sweat lodge dropped from the interest of the general population that had been previously unconcerned about us. The outside activists left and E.R. continued on with his all-Indian sweat. If Paiute attendance increased, it was not massive, and the longed for Paiute youth did not appear. Many of the Anglos felt justified in their claims that the vast majority of those who were most vocal against white participation were people who were not active in the sweat lodge, or ever going to be. There was also some negative reaction among Paiutes. Indeed some of the older and established Paiutes, who had sweated for years - including one of the singers, quit coming completely or drastically reduced their attendance.

The Anglos were very hurt and often commented on how different E.R. looked than after that secret ritual retreat and the consequent schism. He used to smile, joke and be happy, now his face seemed dark, hostile, and unhappy. When I heard about these things in Georgia, it was hard to believe it was really the same place and people I had just left.

As the days and weeks went by the intensity that brought on the schism seemed to fade. The social pressure on E.R. and concern about the sweat lodge dissipated. As months passed tentative feelers were extended from both sides moving towards some reconciliation. E.R. reiterated that the sick should come and others as visitors. Bill, who may have felt the most betrayed and abandoned of all – because of his status as "adopted son" was still angry, hurt, and disinterested, others were reluctant, but small beginnings were made.

E.R. was continuing to doctor in the new way but he was reportedly starting to seem torn between the new all-Indian sweat and new way of doctoring and how things were before the changes.

As time passed on and winter became spring some of the Anglos returned if sick or to visit. Donna and Craig had to move, the jobless valley syndrome, while Bill and April, and Eva rejected the sweats as they had been rejected, and put it behind them. After sharing powerful sacred rituals together for years, believing they were traveling a spiritual path together under his wise guidance, E.R.'s rejection had cut some of these people to the bone, had truly broken their hearts and hurt their spirits.

Finally that spring I got the word that things were looking better for a real reconciliation, and that if I came as a visitor or for healing that I could attend sweats.

I arrived before Easter and found that things had been steadily improving. It seemed that the Paiutes who sweated were never a strong part of the problem, and many wanted the return of their friends. There were three sweats planned for the Easter weekend and it occurred to me that it would not be difficult to add a fourth, making the sweats another four day healing sweat for myself as well as what was planned. I found out that all the Anglos were invited for the Easter sweats, so I asked Eve about it. She was obviously hesitant but I mentioned that the whole thing could blow up again, and this was an opportunity.

She said to ask E.R. and I did. He said O.K. but I thought I could see what I'd heard about; his face looked dark and held none of its normal humor.

I got the gifts and made the preparations as before, except that other people had requested sweats before me and I was not responsible for providing food on those days.

The actual form of the rituals did not change at all. Bill and April, and Donna and Gabe, and Eva weren't there; but the other core Anglos were. Different Paiutes came on different nights, some I'd met, some were strangers. The difference was that E.R. said he had a new way of doctoring, and he no longer called out to the spirits of the mountains and the spirits of the valley. His new way was less vocal, the changes being in whom he called and how, nothing was different ritually for the sweaters.

My journal records that it was a beautiful full moon the Friday night of the first sweat, with a green gold circle around it. I commented on the beauty of the rock's glow. My records do not record details so much as impressions and feelings.

" Strange trips, E.R.'s not doing his stuff. Pretty rough sweat. Weird stuff going down about Eve and her Pipe. E.R. gave Eve a hard time the first round, real hard. I got mad, almost left, instead just kept my mouth shut."

The second day was not much different, my journal records "Real, Real hot - almost died (not really) - incredible how rough." The third day was Easter Sunday and the sweat was very different than the previous two. Eve had told me that even if everything at the sweats wasn't good; healing could still come through. The meals had been more strained than before and everything seemed so different. On Easter an old Paiute named Roy came, and he was singer. E.R. turned a corner that day, and went back that day to his old self and his old ways. He did not apologize.

In the first round he said that months ago he had learned a way to doctor that was not of this valley. E.R. said that this had caused him to lose his power and he asked us to pray for him, as he returned to the old ways, that he might regain his power. From what I've read since, he felt like he had lost his relationship with his primary animal spirit, by doctoring the other way, and following their other advice. By the third round E.R. said he had his power back and in the fourth round he announced that his sweat lodge was open to all regardless of race. There were many spirits reported present that day, and the tingling and buzzing was in my limbs was back.

There was much talking during the fourth round, before smoking the Pipe. There was conciliatory oratory by Roy and Eve, and a scolding but loving address by Gunter.

My journal says "Easter Sunday-beautiful-E.R. back to his old self.

Joyous sweat-spirits glad to have him back-great energy, very, very, good"

When I came outside after the fourth round, and got back in my chair I noticed that my right calf muscle was contracting and relaxing, having a muscle spasm. I called out to E.R. and showed him my calf in spasm and told him it had showed no activity since the accident. It was only a spasm, and I had no control over it, but I was elated. As before I checked for other changes but found none.

It was joy on top of joy and the ceremonial meal was warm and happy again.

The next night I had my first real run-in with the hostility the others had been dealing with. That night a family I had never seen before came to sweat. They were a blind man, and a woman and her two granddaughters. The two young women were supposed to be training to be Medicine Women, but having met them I thought a more appropriate title would be sorceress or witch. They were obviously hostile and unfriendly, not in what they overtly said, just by the way they looked. During the sweat I used the circle of white light as a protection, and was told later I wasn't the only one. It was not a great sweat, and the social distance and hostility was resumed after coming out of sweat, and was never reduced.

Thus my second four day sweat was a very different internal experience from the first; there were many various factors at play. Still I received great joy along with the others at the reconciliation, and had experienced an observable change in my body after a powerful sweat. I had also learned how resolute and unbending the face of hostility can be. I remained in California through the spring and early summer.

Eve was busy, her work was expanding, and her health was fluctuating. Her reputation as a healer was increasing and besides requests from individuals she also received request to come help communities to heal themselves and get through bad times. I remember her being called repeatedly to a liberal monastery on the coast and an artist community in the east. She never charged for any of this, but accepted the contributions and gratuities given her, which seldom did much more than cover her travel expenses.

E.R. had a similar disregard for money always saying you could ask for a job or help to fill your needs but you could never pray to the grandfathers for money," the Grandfathers don't hear money." I heard the story how once Gunter was sick and asked for a sweat. He laid a twenty dollar bill on the pipe mound and E.R. gave him a hard time. He said a healer was not like a MD; E.R. handed the money to the doorman and then they went on with the sweat. I have tried before to leave a check in an envelope on the pipe mound. Usually I would put a cash donation in an envelope and place it on the mound before sweat. I had no other church to support, so I liked to support E.R.'s work. When I left a check, it never cleared, it was never deposited.

I would attend the Sunday sweats and study with Eve and others in her craft network. I learned more about the local lore in relation to sweats. I found out the fast could be used like the plain's style vision quest, where one could pray to receive a spirit power and a spirit song to call it. I asked people who had fasted about their experiences and the most widely reported phenomenon was that by the second or third night inside the sweat, without food or water, praying all night - the roof would disappear. The faster would reportedly see the moon and stars right through the canvas.

By the end of my second trip things had become more like they were before, but were far from the same. Bill and April moved away, Eva did not come back to sweats. The trust, certainty, and ease that had been built up for years had been shattered. I experienced coldness a few times, but no open hostility. I had learned through my demolition work that a structure such as a bridge that had taken months or years to build can be exploded and demolished in seconds. It can never be so quickly rebuilt. Many peoples` illusions were shattered and their idealism dealt a severe blow, me included. My journal became less precise and my self-discipline less rigid.

This is not the place for personal discussion but on my return to Georgia that summer events began that resulted in my returning to see Eve in the fall and then leaving California and not returning for years. The eight year on-off relationship with my childhood sweetheart was declining when we met Eve but our shared studies revived our relationship. That summer, I found that the worst of my bad dreams during my first visit had been accurate. I had been romantically betrayed for on-going months or years of repeated deception, despite all the spiritual posturing, in the classic triangle. We had discussed the possible dissolution of our relationship for years, and my greatest anger was not the loss, but my belief that the deception was not motivated to keep from hurting me, rather it was motivated by her desire for my continuing financial support. I began to wonder about my judgment of people's character; and if there was further undetected hypocrisy in other aspects of my life.

When the dissolution of my relationship was complete I returned to California, seeking the sweat lodge and emotional healing. Peggy had warned me that she had heard of my experiences for two years, had written Eve, and received permission to come visit. She had things to take care of but planned to go when she could.

When I reached the valley in the fall I told Eve what had happened, she was my friend, my teacher, and she knew us both. She urged me to forgive, saying that anyone can fall in love, and to put the hurt behind me. I went to sweats and did experience emotional healing and a certain mental, philosophical forgiveness.

The height of those fall sweats for me was Edie's first fast. She did the two nights fast and I attended the putting in and taking out sweat. She asked me to eat and sleep for her. This is done by trying to eat and sleep for two with the intention that the person fasting will receive the energy and nourishment you will to them, as you pray, eat, and sleep. I slept eleven or twelve hours the first night and was told by Edie at the ceremonial meal after the coming out sweat, that I was talented at sleeping for people. This was cause for laughter, and I responded that it suits a lazy natured southerner.

The sweats had achieved a new status quo when I returned to the valley late that fall. The sweat had normalized, was again selectively integrated, E.R. continued to doctor the old way of the valley, and the ritual was conducted again as it was when I first arrived.

When I left California late that fall I knew that I would not be returning as immediately as I had the previous two years. I suffered from overexposure in California that fall and returned home. I was overexposed in various ways, the first of which was metaphysically. In Eve`s craft network I was exposed to so much diversity, that it reached the point of being disconcerting. I was introduced to the new physics and found it fascinating. The problem was that my spiritual education had been built on certain premises, that there were definite levels of mind and spirit, and that the initiation systems, like the Pagan or Indian systems, were the ordered way to rise and explore these levels. The new physics said that not only could all of that be true, but anything was possible; there could be infinite numbers of interpenetrating worlds. The possibilities posed by mini black holes and the quantum foam made me question orderly progression, and wonder about a quantum jump in consciousness and healing. I faced a possible breakdown of ideation and the loss of old conceptions without seeing an adequate symbolic structural replacement.

I was overexposed to the California cosmic scene. Not so much with

Eve or the Indians, but on every street corner or diner, in any bar I heard people talking spiritual garbellygook and cosmic crap. I heard so much from people who were talkers but not doers, who gave lip service but paid no price, performed no sacrifice, that I began to think the hard core traditionals might be more right than I thought, that the real traditions and knowledge maybe should be closed and secret, available only to those willing to suffer and pay the price. I was absolutely astounded at the number of people comprising the lunatic fringe. I used this term to describe the less mentally stable of our society that are often fascinated by the occult, exotic, spiritual, or bizarre. I ran into a few of these moving in Eve's craft network, on the coast, but it seemed they were recognized as such and tolerated. I saw none at the sweats.

I also felt out of touch with my generation. I studied and spent much time with people a half century older than myself. I had spent my young adult life on a search for meaning and healing, after a wild and streetwise youth. Some of my friends turned to me for spiritual guidance and help, while others seemed to move father away. I had experienced some success in these new roles, but also great frustration when unable to bring healing to a baby brain damaged since birth. The mother was so desperate and I tried and tried.

Peggy showed up to visit Eve and was accepted into her circles. She put it to me bluntly that I had had two years with Eve and if her presence there bothered me I should just stay away for a while. After a few weeks I agreed with Peggy`s assessment, too many things I wanted to forget could not be forgotten without more separation and time.

I had told a close friend to keep an eye out for a good project and when I returned he came to me with a business proposition. He was very excited and it was definitely something different for me. So after a few years as a student-healer, exploring the ways of shamanism, I became a partner, owner-manager of a nightclub in the college town of Georgia's largest university. It was a drastic change. I would have returned to California within a year, more than adequate time for the needed separation, but my business and responsibilities, reasons personal and financial, kept me in Georgia. I had a business, a farm, a new lady, and I just got dug in.

The Second Schism

The second schism occurred while I was in Georgia tied up in business and my farm. My information at the time was occasional calls and letters, but these became less frequent as time passed.

My later sources were Eve's third book, *The Shaman and the Medicine Wheel*, and from conversations I had in 1984 with Edie and others who were there. Again most of my sources provided the Anglo outlook, in this schism the division was ideological, not racial, and one of my informants was very close to E.R., his wife, and family.

When I left California the fall of 1978, the ritual was the same as when I arrived. There was the obvious rise and fall of strong social pressure to oust the whites and silence Eve. When this happened and then was reversed the public pressure did not resume.

The Anglos were very aware, however, of the strong undercurrent in favor of closed sweats and resumed secrecy. Jesus was still prayed to but not worked with in sweat. For the Anglos who continued to attend, the conversion process away from the scientific to the shamanic view of Nature continued. In summary, after the crisis, the ritual stayed the same, with no drastic change in the three ideological question-conflicts. The songs were still all sung in Paiute, talk was still in English, the old Paiute spirits sung to and worked with. There was little difference in my first sweat in 1977 and my last in 1978 when only the form of the ritual is examined. The difference was the schism, the chaos, the pain and rejection, the forgiveness and reconciliation in between.

The second schism happened over a period of years, and was a process more than a specific event like the first schism. From when I left in 1978 until her passing in 1983, Eve probably reached the zenith of her influence as a healer, shaman, and mystic. Her second book was published shortly after I returned and was her first person account of her journey into shamanism and healing. It 'ends during the process of reconciliation. This book was published by Quest which has an association with the world wide Theosophical Society, and world distribution.

Her fame as a teacher and healer was greatly increased. Her new book used pseudonyms for names and did not get specific about locations, nor specifically break the rules. It was not necessarily loved by E.R. and his network, but did not cause the previous out-roar. Again there were people, who talked to E.R. and were resentful of her public appearances, but he told them he had not given her the pipe, and she was not under him or his pipe, and so he was not responsible.

Over the years Eve`s health would fluctuate, and the monster raised his head and was slain again. There were more requests, more invitations, and more visitors. Eve asked E.R. if he would come with her, to talk and teach; his refusal was adamant. Medicine people should heal, not make public displays of themselves. Eve tried to convince him of all the good, all the healing and help for the earth that might come from it. Simple answer - No.

This went on as Eve grew busier. E.R. still let her bring people and it is my impression that after things became legal it was not kept quite so secret. As years went on, E.R. would allow Eve to bring people on her assurance, not bothering with the preliminary meeting. At least once during this time period the social pressure rose again, possibly from resentment about the increasing number of Anglos who came or wanted to come.

E.R.'s response to this was to institute open sweats that were open to all races, and then Indian sweats for Indians only. At one time he alternated every week. My informant told me it went on like that for a while, and then went back to how it was before.

I was told that often the same Indians would come to both sweats, and not that many more came to the exclusively Indian sweats. So things reverted back. The main conflict could be looked at is the difference of attitude between the media and reservation medicine men. The media people thought the more that could be disseminated to the public, the better for the people and the planet. The reservation people thought that what was private and sacred should stay that way.

In 1980 Sun Bear and his woman Wabun published *The Medicine Wheel*. The Medicine Wheel is a circle marked by stones, represents infinity and the great wheel of life. It is used ritually as the magic circle of other traditions. It can be for an individual, or small or large groups. Huge circles delineated by large stones can still be found throughout the west. Sun Bear and others at the time suggested using the ritual of the Medicine Wheel to help to heal the earth and link people with her. The ritual consists of moving to the center of the circle, representing oneness with the Great Spirit, and bringing that energy back to the edge.

Rocks mark the four corners and the circles edge, and rocks are often taken by the participant, who leaves food, tobacco, or some give-away symbolic of the healing love they give back to the earth, in return for all that she provides.

Eve enthusiastically accepted and incorporated the medicine wheel in her work. The next development was large medicine wheel gatherings, at colleges and cities of high interest. Eve, Sun Bear, and Hyemost Storm all spoke at these gathering, often sponsored by the Bear Tribe or Draco. Crowds in excess of a thousand people attended these gatherings held in different places in California, and other cities in the east. Medicine people would speak, and at some the Pipe was smoked. Eve invited E.R. to join, enthusiastic at the symbolic and psychic healing being given to the earth. E.R. disagreed and the ideological gap widened.

E.R. accused Eve of trying to change horses during a ride, or spiritual sample this and sample that. E.R. believed that you must find your own way, and then stick with it. E.R. said that Eve had her way, she had become a Pipe Healer, she had gone through her fast, she had acquired a spirit power, and she had her feathers and stone. She was a Paiute trained Pipe Healer after all those years of training and now she was gallivanting around doing a ritual from another way, and sometimes smoking her pipe in that other ritual, in public.

Eve became known in a larger way than when I was there. She and the other media medicine people continued to have Medicine Wheel gatherings and she became better known and attracted a kind of a following. Many that heard her speak wanted to study with her. She had been given a spiritual name by a Paiute elder and she began to use it. The name Ma`ha dyuni means a signpost or the way shower. The elder meant that he thought what she did was bridge the gap between Native American and non-Indian, that what she had done and become was the way to bring the two together.

Her following increased and there were a few like Peggy who lived there full time. Eve somehow found a way to get pre-carved plains style sacred pipes sent mail order from Pipestone Minnesota. Peggy got one as did many of her full time students. If this practice was known about, I'm sure it would have been disapproved of by the reservation medicine men, who would have asked who gave her the right to have pipes under hers and who the hell BUYS a sacred pipe? From what I have heard the public exposure left her unable to screen the less serious or desirable from her students. I heard of practices such as whites taking Indian style English names, examples like Wind Woman or Willow Woman. Now I understand how the taking of a new or spiritual name when done in a process of initiation can be meaningful. The way it was related to me sounded like rich little White kids playing Indian, and I was glad I wasn't exposed to all this when I was training in the traditional Paiute way.

The old students resented the influx of new people, people called

Eve, Grandmother, who hadn't earned the right., Old-timers thought the newcomers had not suffered or worked for what was now open to them, way too easily. I heard that being there lost some of its specialness as it lost its exclusiveness.

She did not refer to herself as a medicine woman, but she quit correcting those that did. E.R. still corrects, that he is a healer. Eve was by definition a shaman, for she works as a master of spirits. She was not a medicine woman in the true sense, she was not a master of good and evil forces; her knowledge was only of good and healing. However in popular usage there is a strong tendency for both Anglo and Indian to refer to any Indian traditional teacher or healer as a medicine man. The fact that she was called a medicine woman and knew better but didn't say so and correct people irked Indians and some of her old students, who felt that not all the aspects of her success were good, and feared the growth of pride and ego.

Things heated up between E.R. and Eve. they strongly disagreed at this time about many things Eve was doing. Eve felt like the medicine wheel gatherings were really spreading the message and healing the earth. E.R. thought she was turning her back on the right way and was messing up.

It was to be sex differentiation that brought things to a head. Eve had an important guest coming and had planned to bring them to Sunday sweat. They may have needed healing, or for some other reason it was important to eve. She heard E.R. was going out of town and there would be no regular sweat. It would be so easy, she had figured, if E.R. would let her run his sweat. They developed a strategy on the way there where Edie would suggest just that and while Eve said, "oh no" see if E.R. would offer it. The student who heard this thought it unnecessarily devious but Eve and Edie thought it was a good way to find out without any direct asking or possible confrontation. The strategy backfired when

E.R. loudly and adamantly disagreed with Edie before Eve could get in A good "Oh no. This angered Eve and on the drive home said the only reason for this and other limitations placed on her was that she was a woman.

Due to this situation one of the media medicine men came down and built Eve a sweat lodge near Freedom. She already had erected a huge medicine wheel. The media medicine man did not consult with E.R. or ask permission if he could construct a sweat lodge in his valley. They were from different tribes; but this was considered no excuse to the Paiutes who claimed that it was a gross and rude breach of etiquette.

People took sides. There were no formal declarations, nobody was barred from E.R.'s sweat, and indeed, many Anglos attended both Eve and E.R.'s sweat lodges. Strong emotions were involved even though the split was not racial.

In fact, one of Eve's Anglo students went and lived in E.R.'s household for a while. The split was not racial, but who agreed with who.

At that point Eve was past eighty, and had amazed more than a few doctors with her longevity. She had reached into a culture other than her own and brought back something needed, and she had put forth a clear message of healing for the mother earth.

She was a bridge and a way between cultures, and she was a mystic who had served her vision well. She was one of the few women from the dominant culture to become a shaman, and with the gift of the sweat lodge now had all the tools, and was recognized by at least the media medicine men as a full shaman. She had her place of ritual, her tools, and her spirit power, and she too was a master of spirits just like the shaman of old.

Eve's health began to deteriorate with the passage of time. Her body had been ravaged by the recurrent cancer, she had stood up to an incredible work rate, even when sick, and she grew tired. She realized the gravity of her situation, and went to E.R.'s sweat. Hurt, pride, and anger have a way of melting away when the sacraments of life and death become involved. All was laid aside and everyone returned to E.R.'s sweat lodge. When she could no longer walk, she was carried into E.R.'s sweat. When she could no longer travel, E.R. came to her. I talked with one who watched her final days, and witnessed the final reconciliation.

E.R. came to see Eve and she was carried outside. E.R. and Eve talked, laughed, hugged, and cried, and they forgave each other for everything, and they reaffirmed their friendship and their love. Later a spiritual warrior laid down her sword, and having fought the good fight, went shining.

Finding the Star Child

As time went by my nightclub rose and fell and was sold, my farm was sold, and I returned to Atlanta and to Georgia State University. I had sought a secular experience and found one, the nightclub life being tougher than expected, and the sidelines even rougher. I welcomed the return to mental life and in anthropology found a home. I studied ways to analyze rituals, and I studied the Indians of the Great Basin and the Plains, and I studied Shamanism. Three books in particular impressed me in relation to my experiences. For understanding the Shaman as a cross cultural phenomenon across space and time Eliade's *Shamanism, Archaic Techniques of Ecstasy* and Halifax's *Shaman, the Wounded Healer.* Halifax and her concepts brought understanding to me about E.R. and the pipe. He said after I was well we'd talk about the pipe. In his eyes my healing might well mean graduation into the world of shamanism.

Peters' book *Ecstasy and Healing in Nepal* provided me with the clue that the initiation rites and healing rites can be as similar in process as to be the same thing. In shamanic terms this would account for my being provided with an animal spirit. Peter's book also traces the history of the study of shamanism and the key concepts of understanding the elements of shamanism. He mentions Landers work discussing the shaman in situations of acculturation and conflict, and refers to the shaman as a cultural broker. In my experience I saw the shaman as a mediator, not a broker. I see a spiritual and social parallel in his role as a spiritual intermediary and a social mediator.

I became aware of the positive value of my experiences from an anthropological viewpoint as well as personal and spiritual. It was a great sadness that I didn't return before Eve she passed and went shining, but I was nevertheless thrilled to return to California and the Valley of Lost Borders in the spring of 1984.

I drove from Atlanta to the west coast, alone, in the spring of 1984. I had been given ethnographical advice from Dr. Carole Hill and Dr. Ina Jane Wundrum of Georgia State University before leaving.

They basically told me to keep my mouth shut, watch and listen, and be honest if asked about anthropology. I drove to Santa Cruz and stayed with a friend, and rested up from the drive, and caught up with old friends. I talked to a local college teacher who was a friend of Edie's and found out that sweats had gone back to either being open, or for Indians only. She said that things had been that way for a while, often alternating weekends .I later heard someone quote E.R. directly about who could come to an Indian sweat, and his statement was that anyone with a half, fourth, eighth, sixteenth, even a thirty-second or sixty-fourth part Indian ancestry could come to an Indian sweat. The person told me that many people who qualified under those conditions still didn't go, who wanted to be where they might not be wanted. I don't know what they do if you're married to an Indian but are without Indian ancestry.

I contacted Edie and she told me about a coming Sunday sweat. She suggested that I meet her there and I did. I had been gone six years and am a sorry excuse for a letter writer, so I had some anxiety about how I would be received. I arrived early and saw no cars and drove around Paiute land for a while. I saw another couple arrive and pulled in. I met Kay and Vern, a mixed couple, and felt at ease with them. Vern was a thirty-eight year old Paiute who had been to college, spent years as a rock and roll drummer, and had seen the same kind of rough life I had in the nightlife world. He was the first young Indian male I had met at E.R.'s sweat, and found he was from the Two Rivers Reservation on the west side of the Sierras. Kay was twenty-eight and looked to be part Indian, but she turned out to be of Italian descent.

E.R. came out and recognized me, said hello my friend, and asked me how Georgia was. He was dressed in blue jeans, boots, a denim jacket and sunglasses, and looked more handsome and strong than anybody who is seventy-two has any right to. Eva showed up with her new husband Burl, and I found out later she had only returned in the last year, initially motivated to bring a sick friend. I found out Ingrid was offered a really good job so she and Gunter had moved away. I asked of Bill and April, and found that though they still lived at a distance, they had reconciled with E.R. and had left a trailer on E.R.'s land so they could come and visit. Marilyn still attended some, but most of the Anglos I had met had moved on; victims of the jobless valley.

Edie arrived and I was warmly hugged, kissed, greeted. My anxiety disappeared and I noticed the changes time and desert air had wrought on Edie. While E.R. looked the same, greying slightly, Edie's face had become more like Eve`s, weathered by the sun and air.

As I looked around I saw things looked the same; except the wall made of rocks used in the sweat lodge had grown considerably. There were more herbs growing around the sweat lodge, but they were not planted in any specific pattern, appearing to grow wildly.

It was a regular Sunday sweat, and it was also a healing sweat for Eva. She never announced what kind of healing she needed, and if she told E.R. he didn't say. This is not unusual; people do not have to explain the specifics of a health problem to ask for help. There were thirteen sweaters, seven Paiute and Six Anglos. The preliminaries beforehand seemed exactly the same. Eva sat next to E.R. and I took my place with the men. The rocks were brought in and sweat began to pour. There was much talk that first round, E.R. said a few things,, so did some others, when I was next if I wanted to speak I asked and got permission, and I thanked E.R. for his sweat, and for all the healing which happens in it, and for all the healing I had received there in the past, for all that would come, I thanked him for what he had taught me, and I thanked him for the animal spirit that came to me through him, and for all he had taught me about it, and I thanked the Great Spirit for a seemingly miraculous healing that had happened recently in my family. Others talked and when it was Edie's turn she introduced me to the sweat lodge much as Eve had seven years before. She talked about the past and mentioned Peggy and some of those in the sweat had sweated with her before she had moved away. She introduced me as a healer and a close friend of both her and Eve. She said very nice things and if she knew about some of the dark times in the interim did not mention them. By the time we were through talking I was drenched in sweat from the heat of the stones, before any water had been poured, before any steam produced.

There was not a singer and E.R. would start the songs or ask an individual for one. I heard the term interpreter used, and although in the past I thought E.R. had done all the interpreting, it appeared he was looking for someone talented at interpretation of the spirits and manifestations and twice asked Burl what he thought about a report of a spirit. Once Edie thought that a spirit representing Eve had come but when E.R. asked Burl, he didn't think it was a powerful spirit and Edie obviously but not verbally disagreed. The first round was not long after so much talk. The second round E.R. instructed the women to call upon their spirits and relations. That second round as the heat became real intense I felt the onslaught of panic.

This was not fear but a panic of the soul, a fear of being stripped bare and having to face and pay for the sins and abuses of the last six years. If there had not been an elderly woman present enduring that same heat, I would have rushed out; but my ego would not admit that I could not endure and suffer as well as women in their sixties.

During the third round E.R. told the men to invite their spirits and ask their relations for help. Every time there was a reported manifestation it was challenged to make sure it was good. E.R. decided that there would be more than four rounds and before the fourth had the water bucket refilled. There were six rounds that day and they were very hot. During the last four rounds I was surprised by several occurrences. Jesus was mentioned more in prayer and then E.R. asked Burl to lead a song, and it was "That Old Wooden Cross on the Hill" sung in English. I didn`t know the words but struggled along anyway. The Paiute songs came back immediately, but some of the Christian songs had not been used by my denomination as a child. I was to catch a great deal of kidding for being able to sing the Paiute spirit songs and then messing up repeatedly on the English hymns.

I simply didn`t know the words. E.R. asked Burl for another Christian song and I found out that was his pattern these days. During all the sweats at E.R.'s there were two songs in English to Jesus. There were also other songs in English, sweat songs to the earth mother that I had never heard before, and songs in English for spirits such as the eagle. When I later asked several people about the use of English songs I was told to a great extent it had come about because so many of the young Indians do not know their ancestral languages. Many of the newer songs were in English because it was the only language the originator of the song knew.

I asked later about Jesus and the hymns and that was considered to be E.R.'s doing. Taking into account the With the strength of his wife's convictions and the fact that he is Christian, too, it is not all that surprising in retrospect. However, at the time, I was shocked.

E.R. asked Vern for a song and Vern said that on his reservation they refer to Jesus as the star child, from the stories of his birth. His song to the Star Child was in Paiute, and it was sung as though the star child was a healing spirit like Grandfather Buffalo or Bear.

Perhaps the single most startling thing was when E.R. mentioned Wovoka, whom he turned out to be related to. I couldn`t believe my ears; the whole atmosphere was less solemn than I remembered from the past, E.R. referred to himself once as an old fart and again as an old bullshitter. There was definitely more kidding in a more relaxed environment.

E.R. also talked more and shared more of his knowledge after the ceremonial meal than he had before, The woman that had stayed in his household told me that it had come to him in fast that it was time for him to teach more. One of the Paiute men was worried about his high blood pressure and mentioned it often. E.R. told him that it was important for him to feel good, not bad, about what he ate, or he shouldn`t eat it. E.R. said how they say bacon grease is so bad, but how he like to take white bread, sop up the beacon grease, and eat away. He said that because he felt good about it - it wouldn`t hurt him. On another reservation I later heard the advice of another medicine man who said it is bad enough to cheat on your wife, but if you feel bad later and mope around guilty you make it twice as bad. Forgive yourself, promise to try not to do it again, and move on.

I attended four more sweats with E.R. and one at Two Rivers. Though Two Rivers is a long drive, it is not that far as the crow flies, just over the mountains, and they are Paiute and the shaman there are part of E.R.'s craft network.

The next two sweats I attended after my initial return sweat were putting in and taking out sweats for an Anglo woman doing a one night fast. These followed the same pattern as before. They were like the rituals of my past, except for two English hymns and an occasional sweat song in English. E.R. was the only Indian at both of these, held on a Tuesday and Thursday. There were manifestations of spirits, but nothing dramatic.

The next sweat was a putting in sweat for two Anglo men from the coast. I saw this as my best chance to get healing, so I asked the two of them, if there sweat could be a healing sweat for me as well. They wanted things to be authentic, or so it seemed to me, and I told them it would be hotter and harder, but they agreed. I told E.R. what they said, so he put more rocks on the fire.

His healing techniques were the same, the eagle fans still scalding. There were no other Indians at this sweat either, held on a Friday; the Sunday sweat was for their coming out and was also just the regular open sweat. On Sunday there were seventeen sweaters, three of whom were Paiute. That sweat was very intense and powerful, five people asked for healing and it went six rounds. Whenever there are more rounds, it simply means there are more working rounds added, the last is always the thank-you round.

The two Sunday sweats I attended were the only two that really felt like my past experiences. The almost all Anglo sweats did not produce the kind of spirit manifestations I expected from my previous experiences.

I began to think this was due to a lack of belief and expectation - by the new Anglos - for the kind of phenomenon I had experienced in the past. I did feel the old tingling and buzzing when E.R. worked on me and had some unexpected experiences with my animal spirit.

I was sitting and singing the songs in sweat, when where my head had been, I now experienced the sensation of my animal moving at top speed. I knew where my body was, but I was the animal moving, and at the same time, I could see myself as the animal moving. This experience came unsought and unexpected. I experienced it to a lesser degree twice more, but not with the initial intensity. I asked around among all I could, and none of the Anglos but Edie and me had heard stampeding buffalo, or felt the earth shake, or experienced other such phenomenon.

However, the Paiute men at Two Rivers had many such stories.

At Two Rivers I was told a story by one of several young men I met there. He was in a sweat next to his uncle and mother when he saw an eagle that appeared physical hit his uncle in the chest with his talons. His uncle had been sick but got well. He told me once that he had smelled a bear in sweat, and knew people that had seen a bear as he had an eagle. Two Rivers is an integrated sweat lodge. The shaman there is training his two nephews, one is married to an Anglo. There are other mixed couples at the sweat, and the sweat that I attended there was filled with children. There were eight kids, eleven adults, four of which were Anglos. The sweat was run almost exactly like E.R.'s except they sing to the Star Child in Paiute and do not sing in English. The kids can leave if it gets too hot„ but most of them made it the whole way.

As I talked to different people I saw in some ways how things were different and in some ways the same. I was told numerous stories about racist medicine men and political activist still giving E.R. a hard time. I talked to a few eyewitnesses to such confrontations. Once he got so angry at the criticism that Maria had to intervene. The split system of open and Indian sweats doesn't seem to please anybody, but serves to keep the situation defused.

The Indian concept of Nature is as strong as ever and continues to win Anglo converts. I repeatedly heard E.R. talk about how everything is connected, the trees and the grass, all of Nature. Vern told me with all seriousness that when he and Kay reach the bottom of their mountain at Two Rivers, the trees and grass tell their land and their horse that they are on the way.

The real and observable change in ritual centers on the influx of Jesus and Christianity. From conversations I know that years ago at Two Rivers there were no songs in Paiute sung to the Star Child, as there were no Christian hymns sung at E.R.'s sweat. Now there are, in both places, a regular inclusion of Him in prayer and song. Since those songs are sung where songs to call the healing spirits are also sung, does that mean Jesus is considered like the other healing spirits. Is Jesus being placed in a spiritual hierarchy next to Grandfather Eagle and Grandfather Bear?

It is difficult for me to answer in relation to E.R. because the man does not talk metaphysics. I spent hours talking to people at Two Rivers about the Star Child and I would answer yes, a place is being found for Jesus within their hierarchy. They consider him a powerful healing spirit within the context of their other healing spirits. A place is not being found for the orthodox Christian Jesus, but for the Native American Star child.

There is a prevalent folklore myth among many Indians that Jesus came to the Americas and taught and traveled throughout the Americas. This is supposed to have happened around the same time as the historical Jesus. There is a book about this myth, He *Walked the*

Americas by L. Taylor Henson. The figure presented is still a figure of love and peace, a teacher of righteousness.

The huge difference is that Jesus is seen outside of his Jewishness and his cultural background. As the Star Child he is a spirit of love associated with the star that announced his birth. This puts him in a natural setting. The folklore myths picture him as the same being of love, mercy, and forgiveness. But this picture is not the biblical version. What this picture of Jesus - without his historical role in the Middle East - allows the Indian to keep his outlook on Nature, but embrace the concepts of love and forgiveness. The Indian outlook on Nature is **not** that man was given dominion over nature. He should be a harmonious part of Nature, walking sacredly upon the sacred Earth. Man is not born guilty nor does he suffer from original sin. The earth is not evil but sacred, the natural body to be cherished, not despised.

The Jewish background is so patriarchal and dominion oriented, there is no mention of the Earth our Mother, whom the Indians love and respect. The Native American outlook is so different from that of the Old Testament it is not surprising that after hundreds of years of missionaries pushing Jesus that they will accept the Star Child, as a part of Nature, announced by a star, and how he is represented in their own myths, but reject the orthodox biblical version.

My whole experience at Two Rivers was very positive and I was glad to meet young spiritually active Paiutes. I did not seek the four day healing, E.R. was leaving for two weeks after that last Sunday sweat.

He had given me three rules to follow on my spiritual journey. They were

1. Do good; don`t do bad, do good.

2. Talk to the Great Spirit like you would to me.

3. Find your own way; not mine or someone else`s, find your own way,

your own path, a way with heart.

Edie was about the same, she said I no longer had her, or E.R., or anyone else as a teacher. That I was a man, all I had to do, was go and do. I asked her about the pipe, that I wanted one but wasn't well yet and even if I was E.R. wouldn't carve one like my vision. She told me to carve my own in the shape of my vision, which is what I did. I would go up on the mountain and carve my pipe. After I finished it he told me to place it on the pipe mound, on the turtle's head while we were in the sweat lodge – for a blessing. After going through the six sweats and having taken what seemed like the next step, I prepared to return home.

I went by to pay my respects to E.R. and Maria and was warmly received. E.R. suggested if I was serious about getting well that I move out there and live, and really go through some sweats and get back on my feet. Having been financially wiped out during the Jimmy Carter recession, like so many thousands of others. That was a luxury that I could not afford to do at that time, although I wanted to; there were responsibilities in Georgia.

Having brought the past up with the present let me review the present status of the three questions - conflicts in relation to E.R.'s sweat specifically, and what that may indicate is happening elsewhere and on a larger scale.

1) Will the secret traditions and practices remain secret and closed, or will they become more open, will they be shared with non-Indians?

E.R. has been influenced by and also stood up against great social pressure and his sweats will be open to all races some of the time. If split open/closed sweats are what he has to do to satisfy his people, himself, and his commitments that is what he'll continue. Still he is available, the sweats are available, and for those who gain his acceptance, he will share what he knows. On the larger scale it seems that the openness and sharing will not stop, there are too many mixed marriages, and the media medicine people are eager to share. Despite what the media-medicine men do, the reservation medicine men may remain closed and secret, and to an extent may keep a purity of the aboriginal outlook. Two parallel traditions may emerge from one source with totally opposite attitudes about sharing and secrecy.

2) What effect will Jesus and Christianity have on traditional belief and practice?

For people like E.R. room is made within their tradition for Jesus. The fact that some tribes had stories of such a teacher made this easier. Christianity has already had a large effect on Indians as a whole; now Indians may now have an effect on Christianity if they give back Jesus without the Bible, Jesus Jewish heritage and Middle Eastern background, in harmony with the earth mother, as a spirit of Nature. That Jesus may be much more appealing to some segments of our culture than the current orthodox Middle Eastern Jesus.

3) Will the impersonal and mechanical view of Nature have an effect on traditional belief and practice?

No. The reverse is true.

The founders of the Environmental movement saw themselves as fellow spiritual warriors of the rainbow.

Conclusion

The Shaman is a spiritual intermediary for those who come for help. He is a spiritual warrior, and he is often the combatant and the field of that activity, the warrior and the battlefield. As a public and influential member of his community, and as ruler of the sacred space, when social or ideological conflict arises he must mediate between opposing forces. His dual role as spiritual intermediary and social mediator publicly exposes him to risk.

Social and ideological change may result in a change of ritual or a shift in symbolic meaning. I have shown how strong social forces altered the attendance pattern of a sweat lodge, and conflicting ideological forces changed ritual expression. The emerging image of the Star Child is the result of such ideological conflict – a Jesus of the myths called on in the sweat lodge as a part of Nature, a Jesus without the problematic heritage of the Middle East and not restricted to the Bible

Bibliography

Downs, James F. *The Two Worlds of the Washo, an Indian Tribe of California and Nevada,*. New York: Holt, Rinehart and Winston, 1966. Print.

Eliade, Mircea. *Shamanism: Archaic Techniques of Ecstasy*. Trans. Willard R. Trask. London: Routledge & Kegan Paul, 1964. Print.

Halifax, Joan. *Shaman, The Wounded Healer.* New York: Crossroad, 1982. Print.

Hopkins, Sarah Winnemucca. *Life among the Piutes: Their Wrongs and Claims*. Reno: University of Nevada, 1994. Print.

Manners, Robert A. *Paiute Indians.* New York: Garland Pub., 1974. Print.

Miller, Jay. "Basin Religion and Theology: A Comparative Study of Power." *Journal of California and Great Basin Anthropology* 5.1 & 2 (1983): 66-86. Print.

Myths of the Owens Valley Paiute. Berkeley: *University of California Publications in American Archaeology and Ethnology* 34(5): 355-440

Park, Willard Z. *Shamanism in Western North America; a Study in Cultural Relationships,*. Evanston and Chicago: Northwestern University, 1938. Print.

Peters, Larry. *Ecstasy and Healing in Nepal: An Ethnopsychiatric Study of Tamang Shamanism*. Malibu, CA: Undena Publications, 1981. Print.

Siskin, Edgar E. *Washo Shamans and Peyotists: Religious Conflict in an American Indian Tribe*. Salt Lake City, UT: University of Utah, 1983. Print.

Steward, Julian H. "Ethnography of the Owens Valley Paiute." *University of California Publications in American Archaeology and Ethnology* 33.3 (1933): 233-350. Print.

Steward, Julian H. *Panatübiji': An Owens Valley Paiute*. Vol. 6. Washington: United States Government Printing Office, 1938. Print.

Trenholm, Virginia Cole. *The Arapahoes: Our People*. Norman: University of Oklahoma, 1986. Print.

Wheat, Margaret M. *Survival Arts of the Primitive Paiutes*. Reno: University of Nevada, 1967. Print.

www.ingramcontent.com/pod-product-compliance
Lightning Source LLC
Chambersburg PA
CBHW080423230426
43662CB00015B/2194